PERFECTIONISM WORKBOOK

A NO-NONSENSE PERFECTIONISM SELF-HELP GUIDE TO QUIET OVERTHINKING, EASE ANXIETY, AND FIND PEACE OF MIND

TALI MOSS

Copyright © 2025 Tali Moss

All rights reserved.

No part of this publication may be copied, reproduced, distributed, stored in a retrieval system, or transmitted in any form or by any means—electronic, mechanical, photocopying, recording, scanning, or otherwise—without the express written permission of the author, except as permitted by United States copyright law. Brief quotations may be used in reviews, articles, or academic references provided full attribution is given.

This publication is intended for personal use only. No part of this work may be shared, sold, uploaded to websites or file-sharing platforms, or otherwise disseminated without prior written consent from the author. Unauthorized reproduction or distribution constitutes copyright infringement and may result in legal action.

This is a work of nonfiction. While every effort has been made to ensure the accuracy of the content, it is provided for informational purposes only and is not intended as legal, therapeutic, or professional advice. The author assumes no responsibility for any actions taken based on the contents of this book.

All characters, examples, and scenarios described within are either used with permission, fictitious, or generalized for educational purposes. Any resemblance to real persons, living or dead, or real events is purely coincidental unless otherwise stated.

CONTENTS

INTRODUCTION: The Setup 7
PART 1: THE LIE OF PERFECT 13
   CHAPTER 1: Why "Doing It Right" Is Wrecking Your Peace 15
   CHAPTER 2: Filters, Facades, and the Fantasy Trap 39
   CHAPTER 3: The Perfectionist Mask 61
PART 2: THE ROOTS THAT BUILT IT 77
   CHAPTER 4: Childhood, Praise, and Pressure 79
   CHAPTER 5: The Science of Shame and Performance 95
   CHAPTER 6: The Identity Tangle 113
PART 3: THE UNLEARNING 135
   CHAPTER 7: The Brave Day Challenge 137
   CHAPTER 8: Letting Go Without Giving Up 149
   CHAPTER 9: Rewiring the Pattern 169
PART 4: FREEDOM 195
   CHAPTER 10: You're the Judge Now 197
   CHAPTER 11: Where To From Here? 211
CONCLUSION: You Were Never Broken 223
   Author's Note 227
   References 231

INTRODUCTION:

THE SETUP

Read This If You're Tired of Trying to Be Good Enough

You know that feeling when your whole body is tired but your brain still insists on going twelve rounds with itself about something you said in a meeting three days ago? Or when you finally lie down to rest, only to start mentally replaying the way you replied to an email — not because it was wrong, but because it maybe wasn't... umm.. perfect?

Yeah. That.

Perfectionism isn't just about wanting things to be neat. It's not about color-coded calendars or organizing your spices alphabetically (though... respect, if that's your thing). It's about the **anxiety** that tightens around your ribcage when you don't meet your own impossible standard. It's the voice in your head that says "That's not good enough" before you even finish the sentence, the project, the text, or the f*cking *thought*.

And the world applauds you for it.

You're the reliable one. The one who never drops the ball. The one who gets asked to stay late or fix other people's shit because "you'll do it right." You probably get praised for your high standards and attention to detail, which only reinforces the trap: the better you perform, the more it becomes who you are — and the scarier it feels to drop the mask.

You're not just trying to do well. You're trying to be uncriticizable. Unf*ckupable. Flawless in a world that rewards curated illusions and punishes being real.

No pressure, right?

I wrote this book because I know that loop intimately. I lived it. And if I'm honest, parts of me still do.

I was the straight-A kid who thought rest was for people who weren't working hard enough. I learned early that approval came from performance, and that love often arrived with conditions — usually shaped like gold stars, certificates, or compliments about how mature and "put-together" I was. I got really good at being put-together. I also got really good at burnout, anxiety, obsessive rumination, and avoiding anything where I might not immediately excel. If it wasn't going to be perfect, I didn't even want to try.

And that's the real tragedy of perfectionism. It doesn't just make you suffer — it makes your life smaller. It makes the whole world smaller.

You avoid. You delay. You tweak endlessly. You hold back parts of yourself. You say what sounds right instead of what feels true. You look confident on the outside while slowly imploding on the inside. You shrink the edges of your life down to what you can control, what you can master, what you can predict — and you call that success.

But it's not success. It's a performance.

And it's exhausting.

This book is not going to tell you to just "let go" or "stop caring so much." If that worked, you wouldn't be reading this. You've probably already tried to chill out, only to spiral harder because *even relaxing didn't feel productive*. I'm not going to ask you to throw away your ambition or pretend you don't want to do well. I get it. You want to feel proud of yourself — not just survive.

And here's the shift: You're allowed to be proud of yourself even when the dishes aren't done. Even when the chapter isn't polished. Even when you posted that Instagram reel and then cringed and wanted to delete it an hour later. Even when you don't do it all, or do it right, or do it at all.

You are allowed to take up space as an unfinished, imperfect human being who's still worthy of rest, love, freedom, and joy — not *once you've earned it*, but right now, exactly **as you are**.

I don't say that from a place of spiritual fluff or toxic positivity. I say it because I've lived the other way, and I know how damn hard it is to breathe when your self-worth is constantly hanging in the balance of your latest effort.

Here's what this book is:

- It's a sledgehammer for the pedestal you keep putting yourself on — the one that breaks your back every time you try to stay on top of it.

- It's a mirror that won't lie to you — but also won't punish you for what it sees.

- It's a manual, a rant, a permission slip, a journal, a high-five, and sometimes a kick in the ass.

We're going to break down the roots of perfectionism — where it comes from, how it shows up, and why it feels so damn hard to let go. We'll talk about the masks we wear and the anxiety that drives them. We'll look at childhood wounds, internalized expectations, and what happens in your nervous system when your brain interprets imperfection as danger. (Yes, there will be some gentle neuroscience — don't worry, I'll make it bite-sized and swear-friendly.)

We'll also laugh, probably cry, and do some strange little activities that might make you roll your eyes at first — until you realize you're suddenly breathing deeper, showing up more freely, and caring less about being flawless and more about being *f*cking real*.

I'm not perfect — and this book won't be either. There might be swear word, digressions and repetitions. But I promise you this: it will be honest. It will be human. And it will meet you exactly where you are — whether you're in your pajamas on the couch or panic-scrolling at 3 a.m. trying to find your next breakthrough.

You're just tired. And underneath the polished shell is someone who wants to live louder, messier, freer, and more fully — without the constant pressure to earn your own damn existence.

So let's do just that.

Let's be brave, imperfect, powerful humans who show up — not because we're flawless, but because we're done hiding.

Ready?

Let's begin.

PART 1:

THE LIE OF PERFECT

CHAPTER 1:

WHY "DOING IT RIGHT" IS WRECKING YOUR PEACE

Perfectionism isn't ambition. It's fear in a power suit.

You don't wake up in the morning and announce, "Today, I shall be a perfectionist." That's not how it works. It's sneakier than that. You just wake up with that familiar weight already pressing down on your chest — the quiet pressure to be "on," to be efficient, productive, agreeable, polished, better. You roll out of bed already slightly behind. Behind what? You're not exactly sure. Just… behind.

And then it begins. The mental to-do list that somehow always regenerates like a hydra every time you cross one thing off. You brush your teeth while worrying you haven't called your friend back. You open your laptop and already feel guilt about the unread emails. You post something online and then spend the next hour second-guessing whether it was too much, too vague, too try-hard, too *not-you*.

You tell yourself you're just trying to "do your best."

But what you're really doing is trying to not get it wrong.

Perfectionism wears a lot of disguises — and one of its sneakiest is pretending it's just "high standards." **But standards don't steal your peace. Perfectionism does.** Perfectionism whispers that the moment you let your guard down — the second you stop obsessing over getting it just right — everything will collapse. You'll be exposed. Criticized. Rejected. Or worse, *invisible*.

So you keep tweaking. Editing. Overthinking. You write the email, then re-read it three times before sending it. Then re-read it *again* after you've sent it, just to make sure it wasn't secretly terrible.

You spend 45 minutes choosing a birthday card for your mum because it has to be the *perfect* combination of meaningful, witty, and emotionally literate. God forbid you choose one that makes her cry the wrong kind of tears.

You second-guess the text. You triple-check your tone. You fix your makeup *again* even though no one else would notice the difference. You take on that extra project at work, even though you're already drowning, because saying no would feel like failure. Or worse — it might make someone think you're not capable.

And the kicker is... most people around you don't even notice. Because you make it *look* easy. They don't see the internal warfare. They just see the polished version — the one you hustled hard to create.

And so, slowly, quietly, **perfectionism steals your joy**.

You don't relax — you pause and feel guilty for not being productive.

You don't celebrate — you immediately spot what could've gone better.

You don't rest — you scroll until your nervous system is fried and your brain is buzzing with other people's curated lives, while you feel like yours is a Pinterest board of abandoned projects and dusty ambitions.

You tell yourself, "If I just do it right, then I'll finally feel okay."

But the peace never comes.

Perfectionism isn't about doing things well. It's about *trying to feel safe*. **It's about control.** Control of outcomes, of how others see you, of your environment, of yourself. It's the brain's attempt to pre-empt judgment, disappointment, and shame before they can get close enough to sting.

The irony? The very thing you're doing to feel safe — to protect your peace — is the thing that's chewing it up from the inside.

Because you're never *done*. Never finished. Never relaxed. There's always a loose thread, a missed call, an unread notification, an unanswered message, an "I could've worded that better." You're constantly mid-audit of your own existence. And it's exhausting.

You might think, "But I need that pressure. I wouldn't be where I am without it."

Maybe. But at what cost?

Is being "on top of things" worth being disconnected from your body, your relationships, your joy?

Is being reliable worth abandoning your own needs for sleep, space, or softness?

Is chasing flawless performance worth never feeling proud — just relieved that you weren't found out?

Look, I'm not here to rip the ambition out of your hands. I know you want to do well. So do I. This book isn't about throwing away your dreams and slapping some glitter on your messy parts and pretending you don't care.

This is about reclaiming *peace*. Reclaiming your time. Your energy. Your actual, breathing human self who doesn't need to be hypervigilant every damn minute to earn their right to exist.

It's about recognizing that the real flex isn't doing it all perfectly. It's **doing it imperfectly and choosing not to spiral**. It's being okay with "good enough." It's recognizing when your nervous system is fried and walking away *before* your body forces you to crash.

Doing it "right" is a trap. Because the version of "right" you've been chasing was never built by you in the first place. It was built by your parents. Your teachers. Social media. Your ex. That one boss who shamed you in front of your team. The internalized voice that tells you your value is conditional.

You might be wondering: if I stop doing everything "right," won't everything fall apart?

It's a fair question. And it's exactly the fear perfectionism feeds on: the idea that if you loosen your grip even slightly, the whole damn ship will sink. That if you don't do everything yourself — perfectly, efficiently, proactively — then you'll drop a ball, someone will be disappointed, you'll look incompetent, and the shame spiral will begin.

But that fear is built on a lie: the belief that your worth is tied to your performance.

Here's what perfectionism never tells you: the goalpost always moves. The more you do, the more people expect. The cleaner your image, the more terrifying it becomes to let anyone see behind it. The higher your output, the less grace you're offered when you're human.

So what do you do?

You hide. You don't delegate, because no one will do it right. You don't speak up when you're overwhelmed, because you're the "together" one. You don't let your friends know you're struggling, because you've built an identity around being strong, capable, chill. (A fun little trifecta of emotional suppression.)

And all the while, perfectionism keeps whispering, "Just a little more. Then you can rest."

But the rest never comes. Because the price of "doing it right" is your peace. And often, your relationships. Your spontaneity. Your sleep. Your health. Your actual f*cking life.

Let me say something that perfectionism will hate:

Good enough is enough.

Say it again, out loud if you can stomach it: **Good enough is enough.**

That email you already spent 20 minutes on? Send it. That project that's at 85%? Submit it. That text that isn't perfectly witty or warm or emotionally bulletproof? Hit send anyway.

Start practicing the art of "done." Not "perfect." Not "bulletproof." Just… *done.*

Done frees you. Done lets you breathe. Done gives you your time back.

Perfectionism is a time thief. It disguises itself as excellence, but it's actually just anxiety in drag. It chews up your energy in the pursuit of control and leaves you burned out, bitter, and silently resentful of everyone who seems to just live their damn life without overthinking every step.

You know the type — the people who leave parties without doing the emotional math of whether their exit was too abrupt, too cold, too weird. The people who speak without rehearsing in their heads ten times. The people who say "I don't know" without cringing. The ones who wear mismatched socks and don't care. They're not sloppy. They're free.

You deserve that kind of peace. But peace won't come from mastering your image. It'll come from slowly, deliberately choosing not to.

That's the part they don't tell you about healing perfectionism: it's not about doing everything differently all at once. It's about **noticing the micro-moments** where your body tightens, your brain spins, your impulse to fix or hide or polish kicks in — and deciding to pause instead.

Just a pause. A breath. A beat between the impulse and the action.

That pause is where the magic happens. It's where a new story gets written — one that doesn't end with you compulsively doing more, being more, pleasing more.

And yeah, it's going to feel weird at first. Maybe even wrong. You'll feel guilty for doing less, for saying no, for letting things be "unfinished" or "meh." It's just your nervous system adjusting to not being in a constant state of over-performance.

Let it recalibrate.

Let things be imperfect.

Let someone misunderstand you.

Let the post sit at four likes.

Let your kitchen be messy while you rest.

Let the voice in your head scream for a minute — and ignore it.

You don't have to be flawless to be lovable. You don't have to be on top of things to be safe or be impressive to be respected.

You just have to be *honest*.

Here's a small, practical shift you can try starting today:

Create a "F*ck It" List.

Seriously. A list of things you're going to let slide — today, this week, this month.

Examples:

- Not replying to that one email until tomorrow.
- Posting the thing without rewatching it ten times.
- Letting someone else screw up the group project and not fixing it.
- Wearing the outfit that's comfy, not flattering.
- Leaving the dishes and sitting with your tea like a whole damn goddess.

Make the list. Start small. Add to it.

Then — do it again. And again.

Repetition is how the perfectionist brain learns to trust a new reality. That you didn't fall apart. That the world didn't end. That you're still worthy, even if the spelling was off or the salad came out soggy.

You're not weak for wanting rest or flaky for wanting freedom.

You're not less because you said "that's enough" instead of "what more can I do?"

You're just finally giving your nervous system what it's been begging for.

So here's your permission slip:

You're allowed to stop trying to do it all right. You're allowed to f*ck it up, and still be enough. You're allowed to choose peace over perfection.

And if that feels scary... good.

That means you're finally getting somewhere.

The Hidden Cost: Anxiety, Procrastination, Burnout, Shame

Perfectionism doesn't always look like hyper-productivity. Sometimes it looks like nothing.

Nothing written. Nothing started. Nothing sent, submitted, spoken, shared. Just that weird in-between state where you *want* to do something, but your body won't move and your brain won't shut up. So you sit there — frozen, buzzing with guilt and dread — mentally flogging yourself for not doing the thing you already feel too ashamed to begin.

That's the part people 'forget to mention' when they glorify perfectionism. They talk about the effort, the discipline, the "drive for excellence." But they don't talk about the paralysis. The migraines. The chest tightness. The hours lost to self-flagellation over an unfinished draft or a late response or a missed workout.

They don't talk about the sheer *volume* of mental noise required to maintain the illusion that you have your shit together.

Or the physical toll.

Perfectionism doesn't just live in your mind — it lives in your body.

It lives in your jaw that never unclenches. In your shoulder blades, pulled up tight like you're permanently bracing for impact. In the tightness in your throat when someone praises you and you can't fully receive it because you know you "could've done better."

It lives in your stomach — the place where the stress metabolizes as nausea, or bloating, or that weird gnawing emptiness that makes you reach for food or caffeine or another productivity hack to keep going.

It shows up in how you breathe: shallow, fast, upper chest only. As if your body is convinced you're about to be ambushed by a tiger. Except the tiger is your unread inbox.

The cost of perfectionism is so normalized — so *invisible* — that many of us don't even recognize it as suffering. We just think this is what adulthood is: stress, tension, deadlines, chronic overthinking, and guilt as a lifestyle.

But it's not. It's just what happens when perfectionism runs the show long enough that **your baseline becomes panic.**

And eventually, the system cracks.

For some, it looks like anxiety — always on edge, always scanning for something to fix or prevent or improve. Like your brain is running twenty-five tabs at once and none of them are loading. You get stuck in "almost" mode: almost sending the email, almost launching the thing, almost replying, almost starting. But you're too scared to begin and too ashamed to rest.

For others, it shows up as procrastination. You tell yourself you're lazy, or flaky, or broken. You make jokes about your "chaotic energy" to cover up the fact that you feel paralyzed by the weight of having to do everything perfectly the first time. So instead, you avoid. You wait. You distract yourself with productivity-adjacent tasks like color-coding your folders or re-writing your to-do list for the fifth time.

You might even convince yourself you work better under pressure — when really, pressure is just the only time your perfectionism finally surrenders to urgency.

And then there's burnout. Not just the classic tired-all-the-time, need-a-vacation kind. I'm talking about the existential burnout that comes from constantly performing a version of yourself that is palatable, competent, non-threatening, high-functioning, selfless, impressive. The kind of burnout that makes you fantasize about disappearing. Just vanishing into a forest. Or a cheap Airbnb somewhere with no Wi-Fi and no one who needs anything from you.

Except even then, you'd probably feel guilty about not responding to messages.

And when it gets really bad, it curdles into shame.

And when your worth is tied to how well you perform, every mistake feels like a character flaw. You don't just think "I made a mistake." You think "I *am* a mistake." You screw something up and immediately spiral into self-attack mode: *What's wrong with me? Why am I like this? Why can't I just do it right like everyone else?*

As if "everyone else" isn't quietly losing their mind too, but just better at hiding it.

Shame is perfectionism's most faithful sidekick. It's the part that kicks you when you're down and says, "See? You knew you weren't good enough." It doesn't just highlight the thing you didn't do — it weaponizes it. It turns your humanness into a flaw and your efforts into proof that you're still falling short.

And the bitch is self-reinforcing.

The more shame you feel, the more desperately you try to "fix" yourself by over-performing, over-correcting, over-controlling. Which just feeds the cycle. And when you inevitably burn out again, or miss a deadline, or show up less than flawless — the shame comes back harder. With more "evidence."

Perfectionism doesn't fix the fear of inadequacy. It *proves* it.

And yet, so many of us cling to it like armor. And at some point, it *was* armor. Maybe as a kid, you got praise for being "the good one." Or maybe the only way you felt safe was when you were impressive, quiet, obedient, responsible, easy to love. So you learned to perform. To perfect. To outrun the parts of yourself that felt unworthy.

But the armor is heavy. And it's not keeping you safe anymore.

It's just keeping you tired.

And disconnected.

And locked inside a story where peace only comes after perfection — even though that finish line keeps moving every time you get close.

That's the trick of it. You never actually *arrive*. You just keep hustling, tweaking, obsessing, performing, optimizing — in case this time is the time it finally earns you the feeling you've been chasing.

But here's the truth you've probably felt in your bones for a while, even if you couldn't name it yet:

The peace doesn't come after. The peace only comes when you stop making your worth conditional.

When you stop believing you need to bleed out your energy to be seen.

When you start noticing how much of your identity is built around being palatable and impressive, and you start gently, bravely unraveling it.

When you learn that procrastination isn't laziness — it's perfectionism in disguise, tangled up with fear. That overworking isn't a virtue — it's a survival tactic you learned so young you don't even remember learning it.

When you start choosing rest *before* the crash.

When you give yourself permission to show up as a full-spectrum human — awkward, raw, slightly messy, and still deserving of love.

And that's what we're doing in this book. We're not just talking about the chaos perfectionism creates. We're excavating the reasons it exists. We're untangling it from your personality, your values, your habits, your nervous system.

Perfectionism is an entire ecosystem of beliefs, fears, behaviors, and trauma patterns that live in your brain and body.

And the way out isn't through discipline.

It's through awareness. Through softness. Through choosing, moment by moment, to do it differently — even if it feels wrong at first.

Especially when it feels wrong at first.

Because the brain hates unfamiliarity. Even when the familiar is killing you slowly.

So if you're reading this and nodding and feeling both seen and slightly exposed, that's good. That means we've hit something real. That means you're exactly where you're meant to be. Right at the edge of a different way of being — one that doesn't require you to earn your own peace through burnout and shame.

Let's be real: you're not going to flip a switch and stop overthinking overnight. You're not going to love your mess instantly, or drop your people-pleasing tendencies by Tuesday. But you can start noticing the pattern. You can start calling it out. You can stop blaming yourself for the anxiety and start questioning the systems that made you feel unsafe unless you were exceptional.

And from that place — of gentler truth — you can begin to rebuild.

In the next section, we're going to talk about *how* perfectionism hides in plain sight. How it dresses up as discipline, charm, success, ambition. And how it tricks you into thinking it's a strength, when really, it's a beautifully-wrapped survival response that's quietly running your entire life.

Time to take the mask off.

Let's go there.

You're Not Lazy. You're Overloaded By Unrealistic Expectations

You are not lazy. If you were lazy, you wouldn't hate yourself so much every time you "don't do enough." You wouldn't be mentally flogging yourself for the dishes still in the sink, the texts you haven't replied to, the birthday present you still haven't bought, or the creative project that's been haunting you from inside your Notes app for a year.

You wouldn't be feeling guilty about resting. Or spending time with your friends. Or watching a show and not being "productive" during it. Lazy people don't obsess over productivity. Lazy people don't live with that tight coil of guilt winding tighter with every unchecked task. You do.

Because you're overloaded. And you've been that way for a long time.

Most perfectionists don't look like they're struggling from the outside. They look functional. High-performing, even. They're the ones who can handle a lot — until they can't. They're the ones who get told they're "so organized" or "so capable," as if that's a compliment and not a coded way of saying, "You never complain, so we'll keep piling more on you."

And you? You don't complain. Not out loud. You just internalize. You buckle down. You put on your "I'm fine" face and power through.

Until you can't anymore. Until the to-do list becomes a wall. Until the thought of replying to one more message makes your whole body revolt. Until even the easy stuff feels impossible.

So you shut down. You go quiet. You avoid. You scroll, numb out, nap, eat, anything to escape the invisible mountain pressing on your chest. And then — because you're a perfectionist — you start calling that shutdown mode laziness.

When in reality it's a system overload.

And here's the part that'll piss you off if you're not ready to hear it: **most of that pressure isn't even *yours*.** It was never yours to begin with.

The mental checklist you carry around — the one that says you should be further ahead, thinner, more organized, more successful, emotionally stable, disciplined, grateful, socially available, attractive, well-read, flexible, fun, gentle, assertive, self-aware, and deeply hydrated?

Yeah, that's not *your* checklist. That's a **borrowed set of expectations from a world that profits off your sense of inadequacy.**

It's capitalism, childhood conditioning, gender roles, trauma responses, and internet culture all tangled up into a personalized shame algorithm that now lives in your head.

And you're calling *yourself* lazy for not being able to keep up with it.

We need to stop doing that.

You're not a machine. You're a human being with a nervous system and limits and a heart that breaks when it's overworked and ignored.

And yet, you live in a culture that says if you're not hustling, you're slacking. That if you're not optimizing every second of your day — your meals, your skincare, your inbox, your hobbies, your f*cking breathwork — then you're wasting your potential.

Perfectionists struggle so much with "easy" tasks because of what they *represent*. That one reply? Not just a reply. It's a potential to disappoint someone, to say the wrong thing, to be misunderstood. That one pile of laundry? Not just laundry — it's a symbol of whether or not you're managing life like a Real Adult™.

You've been conditioned to believe that any pause is a moral failing. That unless you're achieving or producing or evolving, you're failing.

But the truth is: no one can thrive under those expectations. Not consistently. Not sustainably. Not with their peace intact.

You burn out. You freeze. You ghost people. You spend a weekend doing absolutely nothing and then beat yourself up for it because it didn't look like "intentional rest." It just looked like flaking.

And then, of course, the self-talk kicks in: "You're lazy. You're a mess. You never follow through." As if berating yourself into motivation has ever worked. As if shame is an energy source instead of a poison.

You don't need more motivation or more productivity tools. You need to reset your expectations to human levels.

And I know — that's hard when you've spent your entire life trying to outrun the feeling of not being enough.

That's really what it all comes down to, isn't it? That deep, gnawing fear that if you stop proving your worth for even a second, people will see who you really are underneath it all — and walk away.

So you keep trying to outrun it. With lists, with effort, with showing up, with shouldering the load and acting fine when you're very much *not* fine. You say yes to shit you don't want to do because you think saying no makes you selfish. You overcommit. You follow up. You write perfect little texts and send birthday gifts on time and write the minutes from meetings no one even asked you to take.

But none of it gets you the peace you're looking for.

So let me ask you something — gently, but directly:

What expectations are you holding that no longer serve the person you're becoming?

Whose voice is still narrating your "shoulds"?
Whose love were you trying to earn by being "the good one"?
Whose approval are you still chasing through the way you work, respond, hustle, look, or behave?

Those questions matter more than whether your floors are clean or your inbox is zeroed out or your planner looks like a bullet-journal Pinterest board.

A lot of people who call themselves "lazy" are actually in a deep freeze state. That's a trauma response, not a personality trait. Your body is overloaded, your brain is trying to conserve energy, and your shame is mislabeling it as failure.

So if you feel frozen, heavy, checked-out, or stuck — maybe it's your system is trying to keep you safe from a lifetime of pressure that was never yours to hold.

And if that's true, then healing isn't about working harder.

It's about choosing self-love where you used to choose punishment.

It's about noticing the moment you want to spiral into self-hate and choosing not to obey that voice this time.

It's about making a new kind of to-do list — one with things like "breathe," "nap without guilt," "send it messy," or "do it late and still be proud."

You don't need a productivity overhaul. What you do need is nervous system exhale.

Not to become someone else to feel worthy but to *stop abandoning yourself* every time your output doesn't match some imaginary, impossible ideal.

So, no — you're not lazy.

You're tired. You're scared. You're conditioned to overachieve or shut down. You're trying to be everything for everyone. You're wired to equate stillness with shame. And you're doing the absolute best you can with the toolkit you were given.

But now? It's time to build a new toolkit.

One that includes grace. One that includes pausing without punishment. One that rewrites the definition of effort to include rest, slowness, softness, joy.

And even if you start rewiring your expectations, even if you begin offering yourself more compassion — you're still up against a culture that doesn't give a damn about any of that.

You're still scrolling through highlight reels that make you feel behind. Still absorbing thousands of little images, captions, and videos telling you to be prettier, more productive, more healed, more polished, more everything — all while pretending they're just being "real."

You can't out-heal perfectionism if you're constantly being re-infected by it through a screen.

So next, we're calling it out. The filters, the facades, the fantasy. The lies we're sold about how good everyone else has it — and the brutal impact of measuring yourself against something that was edited in the first place.

Time to pop the illusion.

...but first...

PRACTICAL RESET: Imperfection Inventory

You don't need a therapist or a three-hour journaling session to start seeing yourself differently. You just need to get honest — and then brave.

Step 1: Your Beautiful Flaws

Make a list of **three things** you've always considered your "flaws." Maybe it's your overthinking. Your introversion. Your laugh that sounds like a dying hyena. A scar. The way you snort when you laugh too hard. Your stretch marks. Man boobs. Your tendency to feel things too deeply.

Now — next to each one, answer this:

- What if this wasn't a flaw?
- What if this was just... human?
- Or even beautiful?

Be messy. Be raw. Write what you actually feel.

Step 2: Reframing the Inner Critic

Pick **one** of those "flaws" and write a counter-voice to your inner critic. Something like:

Inner Critic: "You're too much. No one wants to hear all of that."
You: "Actually, people feel safe around me *because* I say what others don't."

Don't overthink it. Just talk back.

Step 3: Brave Day (Optional but Badass)

Choose **one way to *deliberately* let that imperfect part show** today. No masking. No apologizing.
Wear the shirt that shows your arm flabs. Speak up even if your voice shakes. Share the weird joke. Leave the house with the pimple. Show up as you.

Then take a moment at the end of the day to write how that felt.

Even if it was hard. Even if no one noticed.
You did it. You broke the perfection contract — and nothing exploded.

That's how this begins.

CHAPTER 2:

FILTERS, FACADES, AND THE FANTASY TRAP

Social media is performance art.
Real life is pimples, mess, and panic googling.

The Instagram Illusion: Why You're Comparing Yourself to a Brand

You're not comparing yourself to a person. You're comparing yourself to a *brand*.

That's the part we forget. When you're scrolling at 9:42 p.m., exhausted and braless with crumbs on your hoodie, and you see her — the woman with the effortlessly tousled hair, glowing skin, minimalist kitchen, caption about slow mornings and deep gratitude, and you suddenly feel like a failure for eating toast over the sink and crying for no clear reason.

You're not looking at her real life.

You're looking at her *content strategy*.

She probably cried last week too. She probably has a messy drawer. She definitely has her own guilt loops and bad angles and fights with her partner over nothing. But you don't see that. Because the world she's curated isn't designed to reflect humanity, it's designed to generate *engagement*.

This is not an attack on influencers, by the way. It's not even about Instagram. It's about what happens to *us*, the perfectionists, when we start absorbing digital illusions as emotional truth.

For even if you *know* it's a highlight reel... your nervous system doesn't.

Your nervous system just sees beauty, ease, success, joy, and receives the message: *you are behind.*

It doesn't matter that you know better. It doesn't matter that you could write an entire thesis about social media being fake. If the imagery is strong enough and the comparison is consistent enough, your brain will translate it into one simple, self-damaging belief:

Everyone else is doing life better than me.

And that belief is a fucking virus.

It doesn't just make you feel bad, it drives how you act.

You try to match it. You mirror what you think is working. You don't just want to feel better — you want to *look* like you're doing okay, even when you're not. So you curate too. You edit. You post the moment you were smiling, not the part where you spiraled in the car after. You write the vulnerable caption but polish the tone, round out the sharp edges, make it digestible.

You try to be *relatable*, but not messy. Open, but not too much. Real, but not raw.

And maybe you don't even post — maybe you just lurk. But inside, you're still measuring. Still absorbing the aesthetics of people who have no idea what they're doing either, but just happen to know their angles and use the Valencia filter like a pro.

You scroll through homes you can't afford, lives you wouldn't even *want* if you really sat with it — but still feel like you're not enough for not having. You see people meal prepping, hiking at dawn, promoting their new project, doing five-day juice resets and buying houseplants that don't immediately die… and somehow it all becomes a personal indictment of your lack of control.

And then comes the shame.

Shame for not having a tidy enough house. Shame for still eating cereal for dinner. Shame for having no "soft girl era" and still functioning in what feels like a war zone inside your brain.

You're not just seeing filtered content — **you're absorbing *values*.**

You're breathing in messages like:

- Productivity is virtue.

- Beauty equals worth.

- Vulnerability is only okay if it's photogenic.

- Your home should look like a studio, your body like a mannequin, your trauma like a before-and-after reel.

And when you don't match it? You don't just feel left out. You feel *less than*.

But the joke is, so does she.

The woman with the dewy skin and matching bra-and-panty set under the linen robe — she's probably watching *someone else's* feed and feeling not enough too. Maybe someone who's married with three kids. Or someone who lives in a tiny house and doesn't have a phone at all. Or someone who has the "softness" she's been told she's missing. It never ends.

Because perfectionism doesn't exist in a vacuum. It mutates. It adapts. It finds new places to root itself — and in the age of the algorithm, it's found a jackpot.

You used to only compare yourself to the people around you. Your cousin, your coworkers, your neighbor whose lawn was always aggressively trimmed. But now? Now you're comparing yourself to people with teams, lighting setups, sponsorship deals, genetically gifted faces, or just absurd luck — and pretending it's a fair match.

And it's not just women who fall into this. Men aren't immune to this shit either — they're just socialized to call it "motivation." Same trap, different branding. You scroll past the dude with the shredded abs, six-figure side hustle, morning routine that starts at 4 a.m., and a tagline like "no excuses," and suddenly you're feeling like a failure for needing a coffee before you can speak in full sentences.

And if you're someone who doesn't identify within the traditional binary — you're often left completely out of the narrative, forced to absorb standards that were never made with you in mind and still somehow feel like you're falling short.

No one wins this game.

The game is rigged.

You can't win a race where the track is made of smoke and mirrors.

You can't feel grounded when you're measuring yourself against a feed that was designed to keep you chasing.

And when you start comparing your real, lived-in, sometimes chaotic, sometimes brilliant, sometimes crumbling, sometimes beautiful life — to a curated reel of someone else's greatest hits — you don't just feel behind. You feel *wrong*.

Like your anxiety is a flaw. Like your ordinary is a failure. Like your joy is inadequate because it doesn't come with good lighting and a call-to-action.

Real life is uneven. It's awkward. It's brilliant and boring and surprising and so painfully unphotogenic sometimes that trying to turn it into content would kill it.

But it's also *yours*.

And once you stop trying to live it like a performance, you can actually *feel* it again.

You can eat the damn breakfast without thinking about how it would look from above.

You can take the walk without tracking your steps.

You can start that project without branding it.

You can post — or not post — without needing validation.

You can let your body exist without being optimized.

You can let your mind wander without feeling unproductive.

You can start showing up like a real person in a world that desperately wants you to play pretend.

And that's not laziness. That's rebellion.

It's reclaiming your energy. Your attention. Your *life*.

And that comparison doesn't just steal your joy — it **rewires your sense of self**. And getting it back isn't about deleting your apps or going full hermit (unless you want to — zero judgment). It's about noticing the moment you feel less-than, pausing, and reminding yourself: ***this is marketing. Not truth.***

In the next section, we're going to talk about what *is* true — about the human experience, about attraction, about connection — and why real vulnerability beats polish every single time.

Bridget Jones Was Hot Because She Was Real

It's wild, when you really think about it — how deeply conditioned we are to believe that being "put together" is more attractive than being *real*. Somewhere along the way, vulnerability became synonymous with weakness, softness got labeled as a liability, and awkwardness — that painfully human, endearing, clumsy trait — got edited out of our stories entirely unless it was stylized for laughs in a Netflix rom-com.

But that's not what we actually fall for, is it?

Think about the characters who stick with us. The ones we root for. The ones we watch and think, "God, I *feel* her." It's never the flawless one. It's the mess. The one who says the wrong thing, shows up overdressed or underprepared, fumbles her words, overthinks the follow-up text, and somehow still manages to be magnetic — *because* she's not polished to death.

Bridget Jones didn't win us over by being calm, cool, and collected. She won us over with granny panties, emotional chaos, unsolicited karaoke, and brutal honesty. She was neurotic and lovable and so deeply, spectacularly imperfect — and we adored her for it.

And it wasn't just women who related to her — men loved her too. She reminded them of the women they actually know. The ones who cry over nothing and everything, who feel too much, say too much, love too hard, apologize too often, and still somehow manage to show up — hair slightly frizzed, mascara a little smudged, heart open anyway.

We don't fall in love with perfection. We fall in love with *presence*.

And yet, we still spend our days trying to manage our image like a PR campaign. We craft texts like we're applying for a job. We hide the weird quirks that make us memorable, thinking they're too much. We tone ourselves down in conversations, in relationships, at work, online — all in the name of being "likable." Or worse, "low maintenance."

And somewhere in that constant editing, we start to lose the very thing that actually draws people in: our humanness.

No one connects to a polished resume of a personality. They connect to the unexpected moments. The quiet vulnerability. The thing you thought you had to hide that turns out to be the exact thing someone else finds unforgettable.

That crooked tooth you hate? Someone out there will remember your smile *because* of it.

The scar above your brow? It'll give you character before you even open your mouth.
Your laugh that gets too loud when you're nervous? Might be the very thing that makes someone feel like they can finally be themselves around you.

We don't need more curated people. We need more *alive* ones. The kind who cry in the middle of a sentence and laugh-snort halfway through a serious story. The kind who are brave enough to show up as themselves, even if they're not everyone's cup of tea.

And yet — perfectionism tells you otherwise. It whispers, *If you could just be a little more polished, you'd be easier to love.* If you could just say the right thing, wear the right thing, be charming without being needy, sexy without being threatening, funny without being loud, competent without being intimidating, vulnerable without being messy — *then* you'd be enough.

It's a trap. One you can't win. And the **people who are drawn to the curated version of you will never truly *see* you** — and the ones who could love the real you never get the chance, because you've hidden them behind a performance.

And yes, this applies across gender. Men get trapped in it too. The stoic mask. The pressure to be composed, capable, unshakeable. To never let the cracks show, even when they're falling apart inside. The performance just wears a different suit — but the cost is the same: disconnection, exhaustion, and a deep fear that if anyone saw the full picture, they'd run.

But the opposite is usually true. People crave real. They just don't always know how to name it. They say someone feels "safe" or "authentic" or "easy to be around" — but what they mean is: *you let me exhale*. You didn't pretend. You weren't selling me a version of yourself. You let me see you — and now I don't feel like I have to hide either.

That's the magic. That's the alchemy of being real. It's not about performing vulnerability; it's about being seen in the middle of your mess and choosing not to run from yourself.

So here's the quiet truth nobody talks about: **perfection is isolating**.

When you're busy trying to hold it all together, you're also holding people at arm's length. You're afraid they'll see the crack — the tear in the story, the anxiety behind the eyes, the full-body tension you've been carrying since you were nine years old — and decide you're not worthy.

But when you let someone see the crack and stay anyway?

That's where safety is built. That's where actual intimacy begins. That's where you realize love isn't something you earn by being flawless — it's something that meets you in your humanness and says, *me too.*

And that kind of connection doesn't come from a perfect body or a five-step routine. It comes from the way your voice softens when you say, "I don't know, but I'm trying." It comes from the sideways glance you give when you're nervous and the laugh you try to stifle when you say something dumb. It comes from the brave, imperfect, very-much-still-healing version of you who shows up *anyway.*

This means you can stop hiding your soul under a thick coat of emotional concealer.

You're allowed to take up space before you've figured everything out. You're allowed to speak before you have the polished insight. You're allowed to show up halfway undone.

Most people aren't looking for the version of you who's perfectly managed. They're looking for the version who reminds them they're not alone.

I know, it's terrifying at first. But so is staying locked inside a performance that nobody really connects to. So is waking up every day wondering if people love *you* or the version you've built for them.

So try this: next time you want to edit yourself, **don't.**

Say the thing. Wear the outfit. Let the awkward moment breathe. Let your weird laugh echo. Let the scar be seen. Let the moment unfold without fixing it.

Let someone love you when you're real.

And now that we've peeled that layer back — the myth that perfection is what makes you lovable — we're going to turn the lens inward.

It's one thing to stop performing for others. It's another thing entirely to stop punishing *yourself* every time you fall short of your own impossible standards.

In the next subchapter, we're going to talk about the critical voice — the one that sits in your head with a clipboard, grading every move you make. The one that tells you you're lazy, or embarrassing, or falling behind.

Let's drag that voice into the light. Let's name it, unpack it, and start taking back your peace from the inside out.

The Truth About What People Actually Find Attractive

You've been taught that "attractive" is a tight little checklist of things: symmetrical face, smooth skin, flat stomach, confident smile, no baggage, no wrinkles, no weird toes. The kind of person who eats salad because they *like* it, has a passport full of stamps, and always knows what to say at brunch. Instagram has turned this into a science—algorithms picking winners, filters flattening nuance, and everybody else watching from the sidelines wondering why they feel like a swamp creature in comparison.

Half the shit you think makes people hot is marketing. Fabricated, filtered, highly curated fiction. The truth is far messier, and far more interesting, because in real life, the things that draw us in aren't perfection—they're the tiny fractures in the glass. The things that make someone unmistakably *them*. That little scar above her lip from when she fell off a bike as a kid. The way he laughs too loud at his own jokes. The freckle constellation across someone's shoulder they've always tried to hide.

And you *know* this, deep down. If you think about the people you've loved—really loved. The ones who've knocked you sideways. Were they pristine? Were they flawless, filtered, or symmetrical? Or were they human? Warm, weird, a little broken around the edges but *alive* in a way that made you feel seen?

Attraction lives in the way someone holds their coffee cup with both hands like a kid, or how their voice cracks slightly when they talk about something that matters. It's in their quirks, their softness, their realness. Their comfort with themselves—or at least their willingness to try.

And here's what perfectionism does to this whole dynamic: it screws with your receiver. It makes you chase after the *presentation* of attraction instead of the actual **experience of connection**. You end up second-guessing your body, curating your personality, treating conversations like job interviews where you're auditioning to be loved.

This is bloody exhausting.

Meanwhile, the most magnetic people aren't those who perform confidence. They're the ones who exhale into being. Who show up with their crooked grin, their ill-timed jokes, their chaotic morning hair, and say, **"Here I am. Take it or leave it."** And ironically, that's the moment people lean in.

There's a study, you've probably heard of it, where people were rated more attractive when they made a small, relatable mistake. It's called the **Pratfall Effect**. When someone is competent *and* a little clumsy, like spilling their coffee or tripping over a word, they become *more* likable. More real. Suddenly, they're not intimidating perfection machines. They're just like us.

That effect? It's not a fluke. It's evolutionary. We are hardwired to trust and gravitate toward people who feel safe, familiar, and real. People who don't make us feel like we're always falling short. And yet perfectionism keeps you stuck in a loop of thinking that *you* need to be the exception. The one flawless person who is finally worthy, finally lovable, finally enough.

So, how's that working out for you, darling?

Do you feel more connected when you try to be perfect? Or do you feel lonelier, more disconnected, more like an avatar performing someone else's idea of who you're supposed to be?

When you try to erase all the things you think make you unlovable, you end up erasing the very things that could have made you unforgettable.

And the real tragedy is, most of us are too busy critiquing ourselves to even notice that half the room already likes us. Not in spite of the weird shit we do, but *because* of it.

So this whole time you've been measuring yourself against an idea of attractiveness that was never built for connection. It was built for comparison. For control. For selling products. And it's made you forget that warmth, curiosity, and aliveness can't be faked… and they sure as hell can't be filtered.

Now, let's zoom out from airbrushed aesthetics and zoom in on the science and soul of actual human connection.

Attraction, real attraction, isn't some static quality you either have or don't. It's not cheekbones or a six-pack or never having to say "hold on, I need to Google that rash." It's dynamic. It moves. It's created *between* people, not on a magazine cover. You don't walk into a room as a fully quantified "7.8 out of 10" and hope someone matches your algorithm. You co-create the vibe. You emit something, they catch it. Or they don't. Either way, it's about energy, not statistics.

And here's the kicker from biology: when someone is open, relaxed, and present, they emit different micro-signals—body language, voice modulation, pupil dilation—that are *literally* more attractive. Your nervous system knows when it's safe to lean in, when someone is grounded, when their attention is with *you*, not on how they're being perceived. Vulnerability signals safety. Presence invites intimacy. And perfectionism screws both.

Because perfectionism doesn't leave room for presence. It's always pulling you out of the moment and into your own head. You're too busy wondering, "Did I sound stupid?" or "Do they notice my pores?" or "Do I come across as weak or passive?" to actually *be* there. You think you're hiding your flaws to be more lovable, but what people feel is the emotional wall you've built around your actual self. And emotional walls are not sexy. They're exhausting.

Let's flip the lens again. Think about the last time you found someone *really* attractive. Was it because they were flawless? Or was it something in the way they moved, laughed, admitted something awkward, or asked you a question that made you feel like the only person in the room?

That little head tilt when they're curious. The pause before they answer because they actually care about what you asked. The spark in their eye when they talk about something they love. The unguarded moment when their mask drops and you see *them*. That's the good stuff. That's what makes people unforgettable.

And if you're still not convinced, here's a fun **activity**: Write down the top three people you've found the most attractive in your life. Not celebrities—real people. Now jot down the *specific* traits that drew you in. I'd bet money you'll list things like "the way she looked at me when I was talking," or "his voice when he was being real with me," or "she was completely herself—no games." Very few of you will write, "her eyeliner was symmetrical every day for three years."

That should tell you something.

So if attraction isn't about flawlessness, then why are we wasting our lives trying to scrub ourselves clean of humanity? Why are we so damn afraid of being real?

Perfectionism has convinced you that your natural state is *unworthy*—that your laugh, your skin, your weird hobbies, your silence, your scars are all things to fix, not features to love. But the truth is, the moment you stop pretending is often the moment people start *seeing* you. And liking you. And wanting to be around you.

This isn't a call to "just be yourself" in that annoying, bumper-sticker way. This is an invitation to stop editing your soul for mass appeal. To realize that the mess you keep trying to hide might be the very thing someone else is craving permission to show.

And even if no one notices, even if it's just for you—it's still worth it. As when you stop performing, you stop abandoning yourself. You give your nervous system a damn break. You get to relax into your own skin, maybe for the first time in years.

That's what makes you radiant. That's what draws people to you. The vibe. The humanness. The *you* behind the performance.

And if that's what *you* find beautiful in others, maybe it's time to believe it could be true for you too.

Sidenote: The Invisible Prison of Internalized Perfectionism

Sometimes the slippery bastard is quiet.

It doesn't need no audience or applause. No gold star waiting at the end of your perfectly folded towel pyramid.

This is perfectionism when it goes silent. When it turns inward. When it stops being about how others see you and starts being about whether you can *breathe* without fixing something first.

No one's watching, and still… you spiral over a slightly crooked painting. You feel your throat tighten if your morning routine gets disrupted. You get irrationally angry when someone uses the "wrong" sponge or you mugs don't line up in a perfect freaking row.

This isn't vanity. It's *survival mode* dressed as cleanliness. It's your nervous system clinging to control like a raft in open water. Because deep down, some old part of you believes that if everything stays perfectly in place, nothing will fall apart. Including you.

This is **internalized perfectionism**.

It shows up as tension headaches, digestive issues, and a mind that never lets you rest.

You're not doing it for validation. You're doing it because something in you equates precision with safety.

Because mess means vulnerability. And vulnerability meant danger once, didn't it?

Maybe you grew up in chaos, where being neat was the only thing you could control. Maybe mistakes weren't allowed in your house, and now you hear a parent's voice every time you fall short. Maybe no one made you feel safe unless you were perfect, so now, *you've become the punisher yourself.*

This has nothing to do with being organized or having high standards. This is about anxiety masquerading as discipline. It's about a body that never got to feel safe unless everything was just right.

And here's the cruelest part: it doesn't work. No amount of perfectly aligned Tupperware will quiet that hum under your skin.

This is what makes internalized perfectionism so exhausting. It never ends. Because it's not solving the problem… it ***is*** the problem. You're constantly trying to outrun a fear you don't even remember developing.

But you don't have to live in that tension forever.

It's okay to put the towel down. Leave the dish. Let that glass stick out of the line and.. shock, horror! expose a waterdrop stain. It's not carelessness. It's rebellion. It's healing. It's finally choosing peace over control.

CHAPTER 3:

THE PERFECTIONIST MASK

*You can be high-functioning
and still feel like you're one crack away from collapse.*

Overthinking, Overachieving, and the Fear of Not Enough

There's a particular kind of overachiever who doesn't even feel like one, because inside their mind, there's a relentless, echoing static that never shuts off. To the outside world, they might seem like they have their shit together: competent, dependable, maybe even impressive. But on the inside, it doesn't feel like strength. It feels like treading water in heavy boots, gasping through the pressure of expectations that keep piling on with no end in sight.

None of the praise sticks. Because every win feels like luck, every compliment feels like a misunderstanding, and every milestone feels like the setup to a harder fall. The more they accomplish, the more they fear the day someone realizes it was all a fluke.

That's the dark heartbeat of perfectionism: not a desire to be the best, but a frantic desperation to not be exposed as a fraud. Hello, Imposter Syndrome.

And so it begins... the endless cycle of second-guessing, triple-checking, emotional rewinding, and mental gymnastics that would exhaust a Navy SEAL. Overthinking doesn't just visit occasionally. It moves in. It decorates the living room, puts on your slippers and takes over your calendar. It becomes your default operating system.

It's the voice that tells you you're too much and not enough in the same breath. That you spoke too confidently, or too awkwardly, or not at all. That you should've smiled more, or less. That your silence was suspicious and your honesty was abrasive. It's a mental jury that never rests, and every day, you're on trial for crimes you don't even remember committing.

You retype the email twelve times only because you don't want to come off cold or rude. You analyze someone's tone in a two-word text like it's a goddamn crime scene. You replay a harmless conversation from last week with the obsessive intensity of a forensic investigator, searching for proof that you were, in fact, weird, or inappropriate, or awkward.

All of it—every frantic edit, every over-apology, every emotional contortion—is rooted in the same terrifying what-if: **What if I'm not good enough, and they find out?**

This kind of perfectionism doesn't show up as arrogance. It shows up as over-functioning. As always raising your hand, always saying yes, always stepping up—even when you're exhausted, or overwhelmed, or on the verge of burnout, because the alternative—being seen as unreliable, unworthy, or average feels unbearable.

Somewhere deep down, you might believe that your usefulness is what makes you lovable. That your competence is your currency. That your best chance at belonging is to be the one who's always prepared, always pleasant, always holding it together, even if your internal world is a damn dumpster fire.

So you keep going. You get good at it. You earn praise. People count on you. **And that makes it worse**—because now, failing isn't just disappointing yourself. It's disappointing *everyone*.

And here's where it gets real twisted: **perfectionism will convince you that suffering is noble**. That rest is laziness. That anything done with ease doesn't count. So you keep pushing, and you call it discipline, even as it drains you. You silence your needs, and you call it maturity. You diminish your accomplishments, and you call it humility.

But what it really is? **It's fear.**

Fear of being judged. Fear of being seen. Fear of relaxing your grip on control long enough for someone to notice your imperfections—and walk away.

And what's wild is that even when you do everything right—even when you're the most reliable, thoughtful, high-achieving human on the damn planet—it doesn't give you peace. As it was never really about *them*. It's about the internal critic with the clipboard. The one who doesn't care how many people thank you, praise you, promote you. The one who only ever says, "Could've done better."

But that same critic who micromanages your every move will never be satisfied. It doesn't want excellence. It wants flawlessness—and flawlessness isn't human. It's a mirage. A moving target that shifts the moment you get close. And worse, chasing it **will cost you real things**—your sleep, your joy, your spontaneity, your relationships, your damn sanity.

The cruel irony is that the more you bend over backwards to keep up the illusion, the more disconnected you feel. From people. From pleasure. From presence. You become a performance of yourself. And while it might look shiny on the outside, inside you're stretched thin, numbed out, and slowly unraveling.

Eventually, even the best performers slip. They miss a deadline, forget a name, show up tired or distracted or human. And that's when the shame creeps in. Not just guilt for the mistake—but the existential kind. The kind that says, "Maybe this slip-up proves that I am, in fact, not worthy of the life I've built."

That's not just painful. That's dangerous… Because when your entire self-worth is tied to your output, your competence, your ability to nail the landing every single time—you start living like someone being watched. Constantly adjusting, rehearsing, censoring. And that's not life. That's a prison.

So let's pause here—not to give you a solution (not yet), but to shine a light on this quiet hell so many high-functioners silently occupy. The mask might be polished, but the weight behind it is enormous. And naming that weight, acknowledging it, is the first crack in the system.

Next, we're going to talk about something sneakier. Something that doesn't look like perfectionism at first glance—but often *is*. It wears a hoodie, promises peace and cuddles, and whispers, "You don't have to do that hard thing. Stay comfortable." It's seductive. And it's a trap.

I call it: the Lie of The Lazy.

The Lie of The Lazy: When Avoidance Pretends to Be Peace

Yup, there is such a thing. It's that quiet, sneaky side of perfectionism that doesn't storm through the front door with checklists and highlighters. It tiptoes in wearing sweatpants and whispering that you deserve a break. And it's not wrong—at first.

You're tired. You've been carrying the weight of impossible standards, of being everyone's rock, of proving your worth one flawless performance at a time. So when the whisper comes—*Just skip the workout today, you've earned it. Don't worry about the dishes, they'll keep. Don't force the writing. Rest.*—you listen. Because it feels like self-compassion. Like finally softening. Like relief.

And for a while, it *is*. Skipping one workout doesn't ruin your health. Ignoring emails for a night won't tank your career. Sleeping in, bailing on plans, letting the laundry pile up—these are small rebellions. They feel like the antidote to a life of overextension.

But there's a point—subtle and slippery bastard—when what started as rest turns into resistance. When the little skips become habits. When procrastination gets rebranded as intuition. When you convince yourself you're recovering, but really, you're avoiding. And **avoidance, dressed up in the language of self-care, is the most dangerous kind of stuck.**

You start letting things slide—not in the good way, not in the liberating, who-gives-a-damn way—but in the slow, sleepy way that erodes your grip on the life you actually want. It's the second week you haven't gone for that power walk. It's the third morning in a row you didn't brush your hair. It's the creeping suspicion that you're not resting anymore—you're fermenting.

And it's not just physical tasks that fade. It's your sense of clarity. Your forward motion. That drive you used to have, the one that helped you show up when it mattered. Now even the smallest effort feels like dragging your feet through wet sand. You start watching your own life from the couch, as if it belongs to someone else—someone who used to have a spark.

The lie of the lazy doesn't feel like a lie in the moment. It feels like peace. It feels like comfort. But eventually, if you've been avoiding long enough, you realize the peace has curdled. The comfort has gone sour. You're not rested—you're numb. You're not free—you're stuck.

And that stuck doesn't always look dramatic. Sometimes it looks like a long pause. Like staying home just one more day. Like saying "maybe tomorrow" for the fifth week in a row. Like brushing your teeth at 2pm because anything earlier felt impossible. Like sitting at your laptop with ten tabs open and zero motivation. It looks like something in you is quietly giving up, and you didn't even notice it was happening.

Until suddenly, you do.

So how do you know when you're resting versus when you're resigning? The difference is subtle, but crucial. Rest replenishes. Resignation drains. Rest says, "You've done enough, and now you get to recover." Resignation says, "Why bother, it won't make a difference anyway." Rest feels like a full stop; resignation feels like drifting off mid-sentence and forgetting what the story was about in the first place.

One of the cruelest things about this kind of slow, quiet decline is how much it masquerades as self-care. You tell yourself you're being kind. You say you're listening to your body, practicing self-compassion. But if you zoom out, it's not that you're nurturing yourself—it's that you've stopped showing up for yourself.

And this collapse can look wildly functional. You might still be working, smiling in meetings, responding to texts with emojis and exclamation points. But under the surface, the light is dimming. You start ghosting your own goals. The version of you who used to dream, hustle, love, fight for more? She's still in there. He's still trying. But they're muffled now, under layers of "maybe later" and "I just need to rest a bit longer."

This is the lie of the lazy.

And if you're honest, you'll know—this isn't who you are. It's who you became when trying felt too risky and comfort got too loud. Because trying again means facing the potential of failure, of embarrassment, of not being perfect. And when perfectionism is your religion, failure feels like a sin.

But here's the reframe: effort isn't the enemy. Performative, compulsive, anxious effort might be—but real effort? The kind that says, "I matter enough to try again"? Hon? That shit is sacred. Reaching for more doesn't mean you're broken. It means you remember who you are underneath the sludge.

Imperfect Action: Reclaim One Thing

Pick one thing — one tiny, neglected, everyday action — that used to make you feel like *you*. Something you've been putting off. Something that, if you did it, would feel like a vote *for* yourself.

- Maybe it's brushing your teeth before noon.
- Maybe it's putting on real pants instead of sweatpants-for-the-fifth-day-straight.
- Maybe it's replying to that email you've been ignoring because shame got loud.
- Maybe it's walking around the block just once, even if your brain insists it won't help.

Rules:

1. It has to feel *just hard enough* to count, but not so hard that you won't do it.
2. You're not allowed to wait until it feels like the "right time."
3. No gold stars, no extra points. Just the quiet knowing: *I did it*.
4. Then… write it down.

Try this:

"Today, I showed up for myself by _____. I didn't wait until I felt like it. I didn't need it to be perfect. I just needed it to be *done*. And that's enough."

Do this once. Then again tomorrow. Then again the day after that. You don't have to bulldoze your life into a new shape overnight. You don't need a 5AM miracle routine or a ten-step plan. You just need to **start noticing where the comfort has become a cage.** And then—one tiny choice at a time—start unlocking the door.

Strong *and* Soft: Redefining What Power Looks Like

We have a problem with power. Not power itself—that raw, necessary force that helps us change our lives and stand our ground—but what we've come to *associate* it with. Power, in modern perfectionist terms, has been dressed up in crisp blazers and zero-mess calendars. It's the ability to crush deadlines, dominate meetings, and keep a house spotless while smiling like nothing hurts. It's grit without softness. Steel without sway. It's the bullshit belief that if you wobble, you're weak.

But real power? It doesn't have to come in loud, hard, masculine shapes. It doesn't have to be fueled by a mix of caffeine and testosterone, and a to-do list that reads like a punishment. Real power is not performative. It doesn't rely on applause or external validation. It doesn't require you to be invulnerable. It lets you be human.

The strongest people I know cry in bathrooms between big decisions. They leave abusive relationships even when their bank account is a picture of sorrow and demise. They say no without giving ten reasons. They show up to therapy. They admit when they're lost. They ask for help—and not as some grand gesture, but as a quiet declaration that they refuse to stand down.

You've been told your strength is in how much you can carry. How much you can take without breaking. But maybe true strength is in knowing when to *put the load down*. When to say: this version of power isn't power at all—it's martyrdom.

Softness—and stay with me here—is not weakness. It's not fragility. **It's a quiet superpower.** The power to *listen* instead of interrupt. To *feel* instead of numb. To *pause* when your nervous system is screaming for space. Softness gives you access to presence. And that's what makes you unstoppable.

Too many of us have confused numbness for control. We shut down feelings, needs, desires, tenderness, because we've learned that being "too emotional" is a liability. Especially if you're ambitious. Especially if you're male. Especially if you're someone who's had to prove yourself in spaces that reward only polish and pain tolerance.

But that numbness comes at a cost. The cost is intimacy and connection. It's the weird kind of safety that only comes when you're fully known and still loved. When you're seen crying on the kitchen floor and nobody flinches. When your softness is met with respect, not recoil. When your imperfect, messy, still-in-progress self is not just tolerated but *honored*.

When I think of soft power I remember Sean Maguire, Robin Williams's character in *Good Will Hunting*. The man was a powerhouse. He had credentials. Experience. A devastating personal history. But he wasn't flashy. He didn't talk to impress. He didn't posture. He simply sat in presence. He waited, quietly, while Will thrashed and pushed and tested him—and he didn't flinch. His strength was that quiet, immovable kind. The kind that comes from surviving your own heartbreak and not needing to show off about it. And in that softness—in that stillness—he wielded more influence than a hundred TED talkers ever could. He cracked open a brilliant, traumatized boy who had built a fortress out of sarcasm and rage. And not through domination, but through radical patience and presence. That's soft power. That's the kind of strength that saves lives.

So let's stop trying to flatten ourselves into these perfect, sharp-cornered versions of "strong." You don't need to erase your tenderness to be taken seriously or silence your story just because it isn't all triumph. You can be both. You already *are* both.

So, here's your invitation: redefine power on your own terms. Make it look like presence. Make it sound like honesty. Make it feel like integrity—the kind that doesn't abandon itself to perform for the room. Try telling someone the truth about how you're feeling without shrinking. Try holding space for someone else's storm without fixing it. Try showing up with your voice trembling and your hands open.

And here's what happens: when you bring your whole, soft, powerful self into a space, it gives everyone else permission to do the same. It changes the damn temperature in the room.

And isn't that the kind of power worth choosing?

That's the end of the the part of this book where we hold the mirror up to the lies we've been sold: that perfection equals safety, that productivity equals worth, that polished equals powerful. If you've made it this far, you've probably already started to see how those illusions have been running your own life in your own unique ways.

Now we go deeper.

In Part II, we'll dig into the soil. We'll uncover where these patterns came from—why your nervous system flinches at slow, why rest feels like failure, and why you've been gripping so hard to the rules you never consciously chose. We'll talk childhood. Attachment. Conditioning. The roots of perfectionism that have shaped your choices, your coping strategies, your inner voice.

You can't let go of something you never realized you were holding.

Ready? Let's go.

PART 2:

THE ROOTS THAT BUILT IT

CHAPTER 4:

CHILDHOOD, PRAISE, AND PRESSURE

You learned early that love could be earned.
Now you're exhausted from earning it.

Where Did You Learn to Be This Hard on Yourself?

You weren't born like this. You didn't pop out of the womb second-guessing your worth or wondering if your swaddle was straight enough. You weren't critiquing your cries for being too loud or calculating how many ounces of breast milk you had compared to the other babies. You *learned* to be this way—slowly, subtly, and usually from people who were just trying to survive their own impossible standards.

That relentless inner voice, the one that demands excellence and flinches at softness? It's not your voice. It's a composite sketch. A layered recording of comments, expectations, unspoken rules, side-eyes, grade reports, Instagram perfection, and childhood moments so small they didn't even register until years later when they exploded in your relationships or froze you at your desk for three hours while trying to write the "perfect" email.

Maybe it started with a parent who only praised achievement. Not effort. Not curiosity. But the outcome. You got an A? Amazing. Anything less? Try harder. And so your brain, eager to survive and earn love, started gluing your worth to performance. Or maybe it was more subtle—like a mother who constantly pinched at her stomach in the mirror, or a father who freaked out over spilled milk because everything had to be just so. Maybe it was a teacher who told you your messy handwriting was a sign of laziness, or a coach who barked, "No excuses," when you tried to explain why you couldn't push through the pain.

It adds up. Layer by layer. Until one day, you're not living—you're managing. Monitoring. Tightening. Polishing. Performing. You're not asking: "What do I want to do today?" You're asking: "What will make me good enough today?"

And that question is a trap.

We're not just fighting our own upbringing. We're swimming in a cultural soup that **rewards** **perfectionism and pathologizes rest.** Hustle culture. Girlboss grind. No pain, no gain. Be your best self (but only if that self looks great in filtered selfies and makes six figures by 30). Men are told to man up. Women are told to smile more. Everyone's told to keep producing, keep achieving, keep improving.

Remember the movie *Whiplash*? That brutal jazz drumming story that made your stomach knot? That's perfectionism as performance art. A kid with talent gets mentored by a sadistic instructor who convinces him that greatness only comes through suffering. Bleed for your art. Break yourself. Then maybe, *maybe,* you'll be enough. If you didn't flinch while watching that film, check your pulse.

Or think of Hermione Granger from *Harry Potter*. Brightest witch of her age. Straight-A student. Rule follower. Obsessive planner. The anxiety in her spine practically jumps off the page. You love her, but you also *know* her. Maybe you *are* her. And while Hermione's brilliance saves the day more than once, it also nearly breaks her. Remember the Time-Turner incident? Literal overfunctioning.

We're sold a lie that if we just work harder, push more, get it exactly right, then everything will finally click into place. But again, no one tells you that perfectionism is a moving target. And every time you hit it, it just shifts a few steps further out.

Let's call that what it is: **psychological warfare.**

And here's where it gets messier. For many of us, perfectionism didn't just come from pressure. It came from *chaos*. Inconsistent love. Unstable homes. Parents who were there, then not. Affection doled out based on performance. If love felt conditional growing up, then perfectionism became a survival strategy. If I can just be *good enough*, I'll be safe. I'll be seen. I'll be loved.

This is where attachment theory strolls in like a helpful therapist with a messy bun and a whiteboard. Secure attachment means you believe you're lovable even when you mess up. Anxious attachment? You hustle for validation. Avoidant? You hide your need for it entirely. Guess which ones are perfectionism breeding grounds?

Mhm.... That.

Understanding where your perfectionism comes from isn't about blaming your parents, your teachers, or the culture you were raised in—though some days, a good vent about your third-grade piano teacher might be cathartic. This is about tracing the lines backward so you can stop them from running your life forward. Because the moment you can say, *"Ah, this isn't mine—this was given to me,"* you also get to say, *"I don't have to carry it anymore."*

The danger of unexamined perfectionism is that it doesn't just live in your brain; it **burrows into your identity**. You forget that it was merely a strategy. You start thinking it's your *nature*. That you were born type-A, detail-obsessed, unable to rest until your inbox hits zero or your partner texts you back with the exact punctuation you were hoping for.

Perfectionism isn't a personality trait. It's a nervous system response dressed up in productivity clothes. It's hypervigilance wearing a merit badge.

And while we're here, let's once again call out the elephant in the algorithm: social media. It's like a damn highlight reel of curated impossibility. People showing you their spotless kitchens, their six-pack abs, their aesthetically pleasing therapy journals filled out in pastel ink. You compare your chaotic, lived-in, pimply, over-it reality to their filter and wonder, *Why can't I get it together?* You're measuring your backstage against their stage lighting. Of course it's going to feel like you're losing.

There's even research on this now. Studies have linked heavy Instagram use to increased symptoms of anxiety, depression, and—surprise!—perfectionism. Especially in adolescents and young adults, who are still wiring their identity and worth through external feedback. But don't think you're off the hook just because you're in your thirties or forties. This shit hits all of us.

Now zoom out a little more. Consider how capitalism thrives on your insecurity. It literally profits off your self-doubt. The beauty industry, the fitness industry, the self-help industry (yep, even this one)—they all rely on a foundational truth: *You believe something about you needs to be fixed*. Why else would you keep buying?

And before you even ask—no, this doesn't mean you're supposed to throw out ambition or stop giving a damn. This is about re-rooting your worth in something that can't be shaken by one mistake, one rejection, one shitty day.

So maybe today, instead of bulldozing your way through the to-do list, you pause. Not as a performance of "self-care," but as a quiet rebellion. A way of saying: *I don't have to earn my oxygen today.*

That's a start.

In the next chapter, we'll start digging into the mechanics of how perfectionism forms in early relationships—and how our need to feel safe, seen, and significant shaped the rules we now live by. But for now, let this truth settle in your bones:

You weren't born believing you had to be flawless. But you *can* decide to stop chasing that lie now.

The "Perfect Child" and the Conditional Love Blueprint

There's this aching ache we don't always talk about—that small, hollow pit in your chest when you realize love in your childhood came with terms and conditions. You could have been the star student, the quiet one, the helper, the golden child—whatever version of you earned smiles, safety, or a crumb of closeness. And when it didn't? You adapted. You twisted yourself into the version that did.

Conditional love is a masterclass in quiet shapeshifting. You learn quickly that it's not who you are that earns affection, but what you do. Praise for high grades. Approval when you don't cry. Attention when you fix everyone else's problems. Perfectionism doesn't grow out of nowhere—it's a damn survival tactic. You were trying to stay safe, trying to earn love, trying to reduce the risk of being rejected, ignored, or shamed.

This is the mask. The one that smiles on command. That triple-checks every email. That gets the birthday present no one else remembered. That asks how *they* are even when you're crumbling inside. Only because being flawless felt safer than being *real*.

Take the classic movie example: *Dead Poets Society*. Neil Perry—brilliant, kind, passionate. And crushed under the weight of his father's expectations. It wasn't enough to be good. He had to be the *best*, and even that wasn't truly his. His dreams didn't matter. His voice didn't matter. The cost of defying perfection was unbearable.

Or closer to real life—consider the quiet perfectionist in your office. The one who's never late, always pleasant, always performing. You admire them. But maybe you don't realize they cry in the car after meetings or rehearse every Slack message five times. That kind of perfection isn't ambition—it's armor.

When love felt like something you had to *earn*, every mistake becomes a threat. Every B+, every forgotten reply, every cracked voice in a presentation becomes an internal earthquake. It's not just, "I made a mistake." It's, "They won't love me now."

Children are damn good at picking up what gets rewarded. And if you grew up in a home where anger got more attention than vulnerability, where achievement was celebrated more than honesty, or where affection came only when you weren't "too much" or "too sensitive" or "too messy"—then of course you built a personality that could minimize the risk.

But now you're here. Grown. Maybe successful. Maybe admired. And yet deeply, profoundly tired. Because masks are heavy. And perfection is a house with no chairs—you're allowed to build it, polish it, show it off, but never rest inside it.

And the problem with conditional love becoming your blueprint is that even when no one is watching, you still perform. The parents are gone. The teachers are retired. The boy you wanted to impress in high school doesn't remember your name. But you're still over-functioning. Still anxious about being "not enough." Still afraid of dropping the ball, even when you're the only one on the field.

Research backs this up. A 2016 meta-analysis published in *Psychological Bulletin* examined data from over 40,000 individuals and found that **perfectionism had significantly increased over the past three decades**, particularly among younger generations. The authors linked this rise to unrealistic expectations internalized from parents and reinforced by social and cultural pressures—a perfect storm for people who already felt they had to earn their place in the world.

And here's the sneaky one for you: even your own healing journey can become another arena for perfection. You start therapy and suddenly feel pressure to be the perfect client. You read self-help books like you're cramming for a test. You meditate, but only to beat your anxiety to the punch. It's like trying to extinguish fire with gasoline. Because perfectionism doesn't just shape your behaviors; it seeps into **how you try to *undo* those behaviors.**

Let's call out the irony with love and a raised eyebrow.

What helped you survive back then is now quietly strangling the joy out of your life. That mask kept you safe when love had strings attached. But now you're an adult who deserves love with no strings, joy with no performance, rest with no guilt. And to get there, you're going to have to do something radical:

Take. The. Bloody. Mask. Off.

Slowly. Clumsily. Imperfectly.

It starts by noticing when you're slipping into the performance. Asking, "What am I trying to prove right now? And to whom?" It's recognizing that not being perfect doesn't mean you're unworthy. It means you're *human*.

So if today you ticked off 26 things off your to-do list instead of 27, or you walked around all day with that coffee stain on your shirt, or you said hey..llow to that board member in the lift, turned crimson and then cried in the bathroom and still showed up for dinner—good. You're doing the work. You're learning that your value was never in the mask.

You were lovable without it all along.

The Standards Were Never Yours: Who Sold You the Script?

Most of the standards you're killing yourself to live up to were never freaking yours to begin with. You didn't design the blueprint. You didn't pick the color scheme. You didn't choose the timeline. You were handed a pre-printed script and told to perform — with a smile, and preferably without breaking a sweat. And if you *do* sweat? Well, for fuck's sake, don't let anyone see it.

By the time you were old enough to color inside the lines, the world has already started handing you the rules. Some of them were overt — like the grade school sticker chart where neatness and "quiet" got you gold stars. Some of them were subtle — like how your mom only called you her "good boy" when you cleaned your room, or how your dad seemed more affectionate after you aced that math test. Some of them weren't even spoken. They were absorbed. In the looks. In the silences. In what wasn't said when you were struggling.

And then we got older. We entered a world that had already picked its winners. The good-looking, the productive, the self-starters, the married-by-30, the mortgage-holders, the six-figure earners, the ones who somehow manage to post yoga poses at 6am, eat kale, and still look airbrushed while doing it. Standards upon standards, stacked on top of one another like a tower of shame just waiting to collapse.

Social media didn't invent this game — it just put it in a glittery frame and gave it a daily upload schedule. Instagram became the showroom floor for performative living: curated smiles, filtered bodies, perfectly lit bookshelves that no one fucking touches. We don't scroll for inspiration anymore — we scroll for silent comparison, and then punish ourselves for falling short of a lifestyle that isn't even real.

And it's not just online. It's everywhere. Hustle culture hijacked the value of rest. Capitalism told us that unless our worth was tied to output, it didn't count. The rise of freelancing, remote work, entrepreneurship — all empowering in theory — has quietly eroded the old 9–5 boundaries that once allowed people to turn work *off*. Now? Everyone's reachable. Everyone's a brand. Everyone's "building something." And if you're not, what the hell are you even doing with your life?

We're all performing. And most of us are suffering for it.

That couple at the dinner party — the ones who look like a Pinterest ad for monogamy? They haven't had a real conversation in months. They remind each other of dentist appointments and silently seethe through Netflix reruns. The dust they're brushing off each other's shoulders is just that — a performance cue. A reminder to stay on script.

And maybe you do it too. Maybe you ask your partner how their day was even though you don't care because you're so damn burnt out you can barely remember your own. Maybe you post smiling selfies on weekends when you spent the morning spiraling. Maybe you "check in" on friends to keep up appearances but dread the moment they reply because you have zero capacity to hold anyone else's emotional weight.

This isn't cynicism. This is the modern perfectionist epidemic.

And if all of that wasn't enough, the COVID pandemic didn't just disrupt our routines — it detonated our mental health. According to a 2023 report by the World Health Organization, global prevalence of anxiety and depression jumped by **25%** in the first year of COVID-19 alone. Young adults, women, and those with preexisting mental health conditions were hit hardest — the exact demographic most likely to be neck-deep in perfectionist tendencies. A survey from the American Psychological Association in 2022 found that **more than 70% of Gen Z adults** felt so stressed about the future that it affected their daily functioning. Why? Because in a world where nothing felt safe or stable, control became the currency. And perfection — the appearance of having it together — became the only way to cope.

We internalized the chaos and turned it into criteria. If I can stay perfect through this, I'm safe. If I keep performing, I won't lose everything. If I show up flawless, maybe someone will love me, hire me, follow me, want me.

What's even more messed up now is that most people don't realize **the script is optional**. And by the time they're old enough to question it, they're too deep in character. They've built a whole identity on meeting expectations that weren't theirs — and now the thought of rewriting the story feels like death.

And that's the trap. It's not just about disappointing your parents, your partner, your boss, your community — it's about confronting the terror that maybe, just maybe, the version of you that would emerge *without all this conditioning* wouldn't be enough. Or worse: wouldn't be loved.

But this is the exact paradox. **The further you stretch yourself to meet everyone else's vision of "success," the more invisible you become.** You fade into the image. You shrink beneath the shine. You start sounding like every other self-help zombie mouthing off motivational quotes while quietly hating their life.

Studies out of the University of Bath and York St. John University highlight that this kind of socially prescribed perfectionism — where people feel pressure to meet others' expectations — is the strongest predictor of depression, anxiety, and even suicidal ideation among young adults. This isn't just a mental tick. It's a mental health crisis.

And it's reinforced in ways you barely notice: Every time someone praises you for pushing through burnout. Every time you're admired for being "so organized," even though you cry in your car twice a week. Every time someone says, "I don't know how you do it all!" and you smile while dying inside. That's the lie being rewarded. That's the performance getting applause.

You don't need to burn your life down. But you *do* need to pause long enough to ask: who am I trying to impress? Whose love am I still chasing? Whose voice do I hear when I feel like I'm not enough?

And if you never answer those questions, you'll keep following that script until the end. You'll get to the finish line exhausted, unfulfilled, and unsure if any of it was truly yours.

So maybe it's time to drop the script. Or at the very least, grab a pen and start scribbling in the margins. Rewrite a scene. Let yourself ad-lib. Break character. See who shows up.

CHAPTER 5:

THE SCIENCE OF SHAME AND PERFORMANCE

Perfectionism isn't a personality trait, it's a stress response.

Your Brain Was Just Trying to Help (Poor Guy)

Your brain isn't some sleek supercomputer running the latest update of Rational Decision-Maker 2.0. It's more like an anxious raccoon with a filing cabinet full of outdated post-it notes, trying to keep you alive with systems it inherited from your caveman ancestors and emotionally constipated kindergarten teacher.

And perfectionism is nothing but a full-blown **neurobiological adaptation**. Your brain didn't just come up with it for fun. It wired itself around what it believed was necessary for safety, love, approval, or survival.

Here's the scoop: your nervous system is constantly scanning for threat. Like a neurotic bodyguard who never clocks out, your amygdala (the part of your brain responsible for detecting danger) is always sniffing the air for reasons to freak out. When you were little, if being perfect got you praise, attention, or simply kept the chaos at bay, your brain took notes. It said, "Cool cool cool. Let's do *that* again." And every time it worked, your neurons reinforced the message like a group chat full of enablers.

This is **neuroplasticity** at work — your brain's ability to physically rewire itself based on your experiences. It's incredible and also a little terrifying. Because the same beautiful feature that lets stroke survivors regain function also ensures that your need to triple-check every text message before hitting send is now a literal physical **neural pathway**. And it gets stronger every time you give in to the behavior.

The frontal cortex, which is supposed to help you reason, plan, and stay calm, often gets hijacked by the limbic system when stress kicks in. This is why a simple email from your boss saying, "Can we talk?" sends you spiraling into a mental montage of every mistake you've made since 2011.

Your brain isn't trying to sabotage you. It's just trying to keep you ahead of pain.

Perfectionism, from a brain science perspective, is a **coping strategy** with a PR problem. It looks productive. It sounds noble. But what it really is? A trauma response in a three-piece suit.

Add to that a little dash of cortisol (your stress hormone BFF), and you've got a recipe for chronic hypervigilance. Your body stays on high alert. Muscles tense. Jaw clenches. Gut does that little flip it does when you're about to get called on in a meeting. Your nervous system can't tell the difference between being chased by a bear and trying to get through your inbox.

If you've ever:

- Held your breath while checking your email
- Felt a full-body jolt from a Slack notification
- Woken up more exhausted than when you went to bed
- Lost feeling in your hands while trying to get a presentation "just right"
- Had random heart palpitations during what was supposed to be "rest"

...your body is waving tiny red flags that you might be running on fight-or-flight autopilot.

And it doesn't stop at the brain. Chronic perfectionist stress messes with everything: digestion (hello bloating), immunity (sick again?), sleep (insomnia o'clock), and even memory (what was I saying?). Because when your body thinks it's in danger all the time, it reroutes resources to survival, not thriving.

But you know what? **Neuroplasticity works both ways.** Just as your brain was trained to hustle for approval, it can be trained to chill the fuck out. We'll get into that in the next part.

For now, grab a pen and check in:

Body Check: Is Your Nervous System Secretly Screaming?

- ☐ Tick off anything that applies in the past 48 hours:
- ☐ Tight chest or shallow breathing
- ☐ Jaw tension or teeth grinding
- ☐ Headaches or eye strain
- ☐ Stomach issues (nausea, IBS, random cramps)
- ☐ Twitchy legs or restless sleep
- ☐ Feeling wired but tired
- ☐ Starting 18 tabs and finishing none
- ☐ Ruminating on the same thing for hours
- ☐ An irrational fear of "fucking it all up

If you ticked more than a couple, your brain's inner raccoon needs a break. It's your system is working overtime trying to protect you.

Next up: how to teach that nervous system to unlearn the panic dance and rewire for peace.

When Brains Break, Bodies Speak

By now, we know the brain has been doing the absolute most. Rewiring itself around trauma, hustling for praise like a show dog, flaring into fight-or-flight every time someone emails you "Quick Q?". But what happens when the mental overload becomes too much? The answer is simple: the body steps in to pick up the slack. And it's not subtle about it.

When your nervous system is stressed for too long, your body becomes the messenger, the translator, the drama queen that flops down on the floor and says, "We're not fine." And honestly? Thank god. Because the brain will white-knuckle its way through anything. It'll keep saying, "We can do this!" even as your gut is tying itself in sailor knots and your skin is breaking out like a hormonal teenager.

Let's talk biology for a second. Chronic stress activates the hypothalamic-pituitary-adrenal (HPA) axis. That's your body's internal fire alarm. The HPA axis regulates cortisol, and when that shit stays high, it throws everything off: digestion slows, inflammation rises, reproductive hormones get suppressed, and your immune system goes, "Peace out."

In the short term, this helps you survive. In the long term, it eats you alive.

There are studies linking chronic perfectionism with increased rates of autoimmune disorders, gastrointestinal problems, insomnia, migraines, and even heart disease. The Canadian Journal of Psychiatry published findings that perfectionism is not just correlated with anxiety and depression but is a predictor for **suicidal ideation**. That's not a personality flaw. That's a nervous system in crisis.

It gets even weirder when you realize the body doesn't always speak in direct language. It goes metaphorical. If you feel like the weight of the world is on your shoulders, you might develop shoulder pain. If you feel silenced or unseen, your throat might tighten or you lose your voice altogether. That's not woo-woo. That's how trauma encodes itself somatically. The science of **psychoneuroimmunology** is now catching up with what Eastern medicine has known for centuries: the body stores what the brain can't process.

Remember that checklist from earlier? It wasn't just cute content. It was a mirror. Your body is throwing clues like breadcrumbs, hoping you'll follow them back to safety.

And don't get me started on what perfectionist overdrive does to your sleep. You lay there, exhausted but wired, brain doing TikTok loops of embarrassing moments from 2009, body pulsing like it drank espresso through a fire hose. Your sympathetic nervous system doesn't know the day is over. It's still on duty. And if you do finally sleep? It's broken, shallow, dream-choked.

So, let's say it together: **You are not weak, not lazy or broken. You are a body reacting to relentless demand.**

And if your body is speaking up, it's not betraying you. It's begging you to listen.

Now, if you're reading this and thinking, "Okay, but I've been in survival mode so long it feels like my personality," yeah. That's exactly it. Chronic stress doesn't just exhaust your body — it rewires your identity. It makes calm feel suspicious, rest feel lazy, joy feel unearned.

But here's the thing: your nervous system wasn't designed to run marathons of tension. It's built to detect danger, respond, then **return** to baseline. Fight or flight was meant for escaping tigers, not surviving Zoom meetings. Freeze was meant for real threat, not replying to "as per my last email."

When the system doesn't get to return to safety? That's when the whole thing turns on itself. Welcome to **functional freeze** — the modern state of being where you technically get shit done, but feel like a haunted shell in the process. You show up. You perform. You even smile sometimes. But inside? It's flat. Numb. Burnt toast.

And the more you ignore those cues — the shoulder tension, the fatigue, the phantom gut issues — the louder your body will scream. Until one day, it won't scream. It'll shut down. Hello burnout. Hello mystery illness. Hello "I think I'm fine but I cry during toothpaste commercials now."

So, what do we actually do?

Let's talk **regulation before revelation**. You can't think your way out of a dysregulated system. That's like trying to do taxes while your kitchen's on fire. First, we calm the blaze.

We start by creating a **new definition of safety** — not just the absence of danger, but the presence of enough. Enough breath. Enough space. Enough permission to pause. You train your system by giving it what it didn't get before: evidence that rest is allowed. That presence doesn't require performance.

Even science backs this up. Studies from Stanford and Harvard have shown that **vagal tone** — the flexibility of your nervous system's recovery response — improves dramatically with regular breathwork, grounding, and somatic release. And that higher vagal tone is correlated with better emotion regulation, deeper connection, and less reactivity. In other words, your nervous system becomes a chill, wise elder instead of a caffeinated squirrel with PTSD.

And no, this doesn't mean you suddenly stop caring or give up goals. It means you stop sacrificing your body to the altar of productivity. You can still build. Still create. Still achieve — but from a state of *capacity*, not depletion. From *choice*, not compulsion.

Here's where the fun part starts. Once your system starts to trust you — when it sees you're no longer dragging it through endless loops of "do more, be better, fix everything" — it actually gives you more to work with. More access to intuition. To joy. To weird ideas that might change your whole trajectory.

Because guess what? Creativity, play, rest, and resilience — they all live in the *parasympathetic* nervous system. That's your calm-down state. Your repair-and-thrive zone. You can't fake your way there. You can only arrive there by making it safe to stop hustling. Even for a moment.

So here's your challenge: pick **one ritual of nervous system kindness** and make it part of your daily life. Doesn't have to be dramatic. Could be two minutes of humming before a meeting. Could be stretching while your coffee brews. Could be a post-it on your desk that says "We're not in danger right now."

Make it easy. Make it stupidly simple. Repetition rewires. And if you do it with intention, your nervous system will start believing the one thing it's never fully trusted before:

That you're allowed to feel good, even when nothing's perfect.

So, now we'll look at how self-criticism and perfectionist pressure warp your inner voice — and how neuroscience shows that shame-based motivation is not only ineffective, it actually screws with your brain chemistry. But don't worry — there's a better way. One that includes compassion without losing standards.

You Can't Hate Yourself Into Peace

If hating yourself into healing actually worked, perfectionists would be the most peaceful people on the planet.

But here we are. Anxious, exhausted, hyper-aware of every eyebrow twitch of disapproval, convinced that one more spreadsheet, one more body transformation, one more gold star will finally silence the inner critic who's been narrating our every move like a passive-aggressive podcast host.

Let's just say it plainly: **self-loathing is not a sustainable strategy**. It doesn't motivate—it mutilates. It doesn't discipline—it disorients. You can only berate a nervous system so many times before it stops listening, shuts down, and files everything under "We're clearly not safe here."

And neuroscience has actually confirmed this. When we shame ourselves—when we ruminate, self-criticize, or beat ourselves up—we activate the dorsal anterior cingulate cortex and the insula, regions in the brain associated with pain processing. Literal pain. As in, **your brain treats harsh self-talk like it would a physical injury**. So that voice in your head saying, "You're not good enough, you'll always be behind, why can't you get your shit together"—it's not "tough love." It's neural warfare.

Now contrast that with **self-compassion**—the one thing perfectionists avoid like the plague because it sounds too soft, too lenient, too... Oprah. But when you practice self-compassion, you activate the **care system** of the brain—yep, that's a thing. You trigger oxytocin and endorphins. You calm the amygdala. You widen your window of tolerance for stress. In short: your brain becomes a safer place to be.

Let's bring in Dr. Kristin Neff here—the psychologist who basically put self-compassion on the academic map. Her research shows that self-compassionate people are *more* likely to take responsibility for their mistakes, not less. They're *more* resilient, *more* motivated to grow, and *less* likely to spiral into shame-fueled paralysis.

So why does the lie persist? Why do we still believe we have to be harsh to be strong?

Because the hustle culture we marinated in never taught us how to rest without guilt. Because the families we grew up in often modeled love as conditional: perform well, be good, get praise. Screw up, get distance. And because our education systems rewarded outcomes, not effort, not curiosity, not kindness toward ourselves.

We internalized a sick equation: **"You are only as worthy as your last win."** And when that win doesn't come? Cue the self-flagellation.

How many of us have gone on "self-improvement" benders that were just self-hatred in activewear? How many wellness routines were actually just control in disguise? Meditating to "fix your brain," journaling to "purge the negativity," skincare because your face wasn't allowed to look tired?

We turned healing into performance. Self-compassion into another fucking checkbox. And then we wondered why we didn't feel better.

So, no: **you don't earn peace by punishing yourself.** You don't unlock joy by perfecting your pain. You stop suffering when you stop believing that your pain makes you unworthy.

That doesn't mean you stop growing. It means you grow *with* yourself, not *against* yourself.

And yeah babe, that's scary. As most of us were trained to equate softness with weakness. But softness is what lets things grow. No seed ever cracked open because you yelled at it.

So how do you actually stop fighting with yourself? How do you stop hurling mental chairs across the room every time you mess up or feel like a fraud or eat a goddamn croissant on a weekday?

You **start by interrupting the story**. The one where you're only lovable when you're useful. The one where effort equals value. The one where your worth is measured in neatness, compliance, and how many unread emails you heroically annihilated before breakfast.

You rewrite the narrative with action, not just insight. And knowing you're being hard on yourself isn't the same as being kind. You need reps. You need to *practice* compassion like you once practiced hiding it.

Start here: **Name the voice.** That brutal narrator? Give it a character. Call it something like "The Auditor" or "Judge Judy on Steroids." Externalizing the inner critic helps you stop confusing it for truth. You can't challenge what you still identify with.

Next: **Talk back like someone you love is listening.** You wouldn't say to a friend, "Wow, you forgot to reply to that email? You're basically a useless human." But that's exactly what we say to ourselves. So borrow your best friend's voice, your inner elder, your future self—anyone who can see your mess and *still* hold space.

And then: **Do something wildly imperfect… on purpose.** Not to self-sabotage. But to prove that your survival doesn't depend on flawlessness. Let the Zoom call happen with messy hair. Post a typo. Burn the toast and eat it anyway. Watch how nothing falls apart. Watch how your world *doesn't* implode when you're human.

And here's what's really at stake: if you keep punishing yourself for being messy, you'll never feel safe enough to be authentic. And if you're not authentic, you'll attract relationships, careers, even identities that require constant emotional Spanx to maintain. That's not a life. That's a performance in a straightjacket.

You want freedom? You want peace? Then you've got to stop auditioning for your own damn approval.

So here's something small but mighty to try right now:

Imperfect Activity: Your Anti-Perfectionist Pep Talk

1. **Write down the last time you were hard on yourself.** Be honest. What did you say? What tone did you use?

2. **Now rewrite the script**—as if you were speaking to a child you adore. Keep it real, but keep it kind.

3. **Read both versions out loud.** Feel the difference in your body. Notice which version leaves you tense… and which one feels like exhaling.

4. **Bonus round:** Put the kinder version on a post-it note or in your phone. Read it again tomorrow. And again the day after that.

It's not weakness. It's **retraining your nervous system to recognize safety**, not threat. It's showing your brain, "Hey, it's okay. We don't need to hustle for our humanity anymore. We're already home."

And this shift doesn't just affect how you talk to yourself. It changes how you show up for everything else. Because when you stop performing for worth, you start **living from it**.

But don't worry—we're not done yet. As even if you're starting to soften toward yourself, that's just half the battle. You still have to face the world. And the world? Oh, it *loves* a shiny surface.

So next, we're diving into the outside forces that shaped this madness. Childhood dynamics. Social media distortion. Cultural brainwashing. Why your quest for perfection didn't start with you—but it *can* end with you.

Chapter 6 is where we break the cycle. Get ready to meet your inner child, your unspoken rules, and all the sneaky systems that taught you how to self-abandon in the first place.

Spoiler: They were wrong. You were never too much. You were never not enough. You were just trying to be good in a world that never gave you a map.

Let's burn the map.

CHAPTER 6:

THE IDENTITY TANGLE

*Who are you without your gold stars,
A+ grades, or flawless output?*

The Original You: Before the Performance Took Over

Before you learned how to be impressive, you were just... you.

You had crooked drawings and big feelings and questionable outfits you refused to take off. You belly-laughed. You asked too many questions. You got grape juice mustaches and thought your invisible friend was the funniest bastard on earth. You had instincts before you had strategy. You didn't measure your worth by productivity or polish or how well your personality aligned with the LinkedIn algorithm. You were just existing — loud, curious, alive.

And then, slowly — or maybe suddenly — something shifted.

You clocked that certain behaviors got more applause. That praise came easier when you were tidy, or smart, or useful, or quiet. You started editing yourself. Not because you were fake. Because you were adaptive. That's the brain doing what it does best — noticing patterns, predicting outcomes, and protecting you. So you sanded down the weird edges. You tucked away the wild ideas. You tried being good, then great, then exceptional.

And with each gold star, a piece of you went into hiding.

But the original you never left. They're just buried under a thousand layers of performance and proof. And it's not about going back in time and becoming a child again. It's about excavating the parts of yourself that weren't built on compliance, fear, or achievement. The part that existed before you were given a template for "how to be acceptable."

A lot of us associate authenticity with some perfectly curated idea of "realness" — as if being real is another task to get right. But authenticity isn't an aesthetic. It's not a morning routine or a detox or an Instagram caption "just being raw today!" It's messier. Weirder. Sometimes inconvenient. It's admitting that you hate birthday parties or that you secretly love trashy reality shows or that you don't actually enjoy working out — you just feel like you're supposed to.

A lot of people spend their whole lives playing the role that kept them safe as kids. The good girl. The overachiever. The peacemaker. The reliable one. The golden boy. The one who never needed anything. And at some point, they look around at their polished, responsible life and think: is this all there is?

And if that thought has ever crossed your mind — if there's a restlessness under the surface that can't be cured by another promotion, another project, another goddamn green smoothie — then congratulations. That's not failure. That's your original self tugging at the sleeve of your perfectionist costume, whispering, "Hey, remember me?"

Sometimes it shows up as boredom. Or burnout. Or crying in the car for no reason you can explain. Sometimes it's the feeling of being surrounded by people who admire you but don't really *know* you. Sometimes it's not being able to answer the question, "What do you want?" without defaulting to whatever sounds most productive.

But that self — the one you started as — still has a pulse.

Reconnecting with that version of you might feel terrifying. It might feel indulgent, even dangerous. Especially if you grew up with chaos, neglect, criticism, or just a vibe that said, "Don't take up too much space." Because your system learned that performing kept you safe — and safety always wins over authenticity when push comes to shove.

So this process? It's not about blowing up your life. It's about remembering the parts of you that got lost in the performance. The parts that didn't need to be earned.

We're going to dig for that gold. But where do you even begin?

Especially when the version of you who's done the performing has built an entire life — and maybe even an identity — around being competent, composed, and *needed*. You don't just throw off the mask and skip through a meadow of self-discovery. Most people need a breadcrumb trail to follow. So let's start there.

The first breadcrumb is **desire** — the unfiltered kind. What do you daydream about when no one's watching? What random thing makes your chest feel fizzy with excitement, even if it seems silly or impractical? That's a clue. Because the original you probably didn't care if something was impressive. They cared if it felt alive.

The second breadcrumb? **Irritation**. The stuff that makes you irrationally annoyed — like performative wellness influencers or relentless small talk or the phrase "circle back." That low-grade rage is a compass. It points toward what you've been tolerating that's out of alignment with who you are. The original you had preferences. The performer version learned to swallow them.

The third one's a bit spicy: **envy**. Who are you jealous of, and why? Not in the toxic comparison sense — in the "damn, I wish I had the guts to do that" sense. That kind of envy often points toward disowned dreams, especially the ones you talked yourself out of because they weren't realistic or respectable or whatever else perfectionism told you was more important than joy.

And finally, watch for the **glitch** — the moment when your body says one thing while your mouth says another. Like when you say "Sure, I'd love to help!" and your stomach clenches. Or when you post the polished family photo but your jaw tightens because you fought with your partner the entire way there. Those body glitches are data. The original you spoke through the body long before they knew how to please through words.

Here's a small but powerful exercise:

Rediscovering the Original You

1. Write a list of things you loved doing before anyone told you what you *should* love.

2. Highlight the ones that still spark a little curiosity or warmth.

3. Pick one and spend 30 minutes with it this week — not to get good at it, not to share it, not to turn it into content. Just for you.

This isn't about regression. It's about re-integration. You're not ditching your adult self — you're bringing more color back into the version of you that exists now. A version that's allowed to be competent *and* playful, strategic *and* weird, responsible *and* soft.

And here's the truth: the original you wasn't wrong. They weren't too much. They were just... early. Before the world convinced you otherwise.

And maybe it's time they made a comeback.

The False Self: Who You Built to Survive

You know that nobody sets out to be fake. That you don't wake up one day and decide, "You know what? I think I'll abandon my essence and become a polished, performative projection of what other people want from me."

But you do wake up one day and realize that's exactly what happened.

The false self isn't a costume you put on for fun. It's body armor. It's the carefully engineered persona built brick by brick to help you navigate a world that didn't always feel safe, fair, or forgiving. And it started young. Maybe when you figured out that being smart got you attention, but crying got you silence. Or when being agreeable kept your parents from fighting. Or when being responsible was the only way to get noticed in a house full of chaos.

That version of you — the one who figured out how to cope, how to please, how to survive — was brilliant. They were resourceful as hell. And they deserve some damn credit. Without that false self, you might not have made it through school, or your parents' divorce, or those friendships where you always had to be "the stable one."

But here's where it gets sticky: survival strategies are meant to be temporary. They're supposed to help you get through. Not define who you become.

When your false self becomes your full-time identity, you don't just lose access to your instincts. You start gaslighting yourself. You tell yourself you actually like being productive all the time. That saying "yes" is empowering. That being needed is the same as being loved. And even when you're exhausted, resentful, or quietly panicking at the idea of being alone, you cling to the performance. Because it's the only self you know.

Think of it like emotional auto-tune. The false self smooths out your rough edges, but it also flattens your depth. It keeps you socially acceptable but personally disconnected. You're getting applause for a role you didn't even audition for. Until...

Until you start to notice that people admire your discipline but don't know your fears. That they appreciate your consistency but don't see your chaos or think you're so put together, so impressive, so "low maintenance" and have no bloody clue that you're screaming inside because no one ever stops to ask, "Hey... is any of this even working for *you*?"

This false self is slippery. It looks like confidence, but it's actually fear in a Prada dress. It looks like ambition, but it's actually panic with a Google Calendar. It looks like generosity, but it's actually a desperate attempt to be worth keeping around.

And it works. Until it doesn't.

The cracks usually show up in weird places. Maybe it's a relationship where you realize you've been overperforming the whole time and now you don't know how to stop. Maybe it's burnout that doesn't go away after a vacation. Maybe it's a birthday where you feel like everyone's celebrating a version of you that isn't real. Maybe it's a random Tuesday where you cancel plans because the idea of pretending to be "on" feels like emotional waterboarding.

That's not failure.

That's the moment the false self starts to outlive its usefulness. The moment your real self starts banging on the door from the inside, asking for permission to come out again.

The thing about the False Self is that it's not a villain. It's a bodyguard. It doesn't wake up plotting to steal your joy — it wakes up planning to keep you alive. And honestly? It probably did a damn good job. For years, maybe decades, it kept things tidy. Predictable. Appealing. It got the promotions. It made the family proud. It got you liked, accepted, admired.

But **liked isn't the same as known**. And admired isn't the same as loved.

The False Self is brilliant — a master strategist that was built out of necessity. It scanned its environment, sniffed out the rules, and then optimized like hell. Got abandonment issues? Be the funny one. Got criticism every time you showed emotion? Become the stoic. Learned early that nothing was ever quite enough? Hello, high-achieving machine with burnout in their bloodstream.

But after a while, the strategies stop serving. Or rather, they start costing. And the cost is steep: loneliness inside relationships. Emotional constipation. A chronic sense that no one *really* gets you — maybe because you've never let them. Maybe because you forgot how.

So, how do you start unmasking — gently, intentionally, without sending your nervous system into a full-blown existential panic?

You start with *one room* in your life where it feels safe to show up just a little more real.

Maybe that's with a close friend who always meets you with softness. Maybe it's in the voice memo you record for yourself on the way home from work. Maybe it's just in how you dress on the weekend — clothes that feel like *you* instead of like the LinkedIn version of yourself.

Then, you try showing up with a bit less polish. Not everywhere. Not all at once. But *somewhere*.

Start by telling the truth in low-stakes situations:

- "Actually, I'm really tired today."

- "No, I don't want to go to that."

- "I don't have an answer yet, but I'm figuring it out."

- "I know I always seem together, but I've been struggling lately."

These aren't confessions. They're recalibrations. Micro-adjustments that give your nervous system proof that it's safe to be real. That you won't die if you disappoint someone. That honesty doesn't always lead to exile.

And here's a wild realization: some people will love you *more* for the things you've always tried to hide.

Your messiness. Your awkwardness. Your contradictions. Your refusal to say yes just to keep the peace.

Real connection doesn't happen through perfection. It happens through presence. And presence requires truth. Even the wobbly kind. Even the kind that feels like you're fumbling through a sentence and forgetting how to make eye contact.

Let's close with an exercise to put this into practice:

EXERCISE: Spot the Mask

1. List three situations where you feel like you're "on." (Work meetings? Family dinners? Instagram?)

2. For each, ask: What role am I playing here? What version of me shows up?

3. Then ask: What am I afraid would happen if I showed up 10% more real?

4. Finally, pick one situation and experiment: try softening the performance just slightly. Not radically — just a shift. A shrug. A laugh. A truth.

This isn't about throwing out everything that's gotten you here. It's about slowly, steadily, giving the mic back to the part of you that's been silenced the longest.

Becoming Real: Reconnecting With the Self You Exiled

You don't *become* real by being good. You become real by being honest. With yourself. With others. With the mirror you've been side-eyeing for years because it might show you something you're not sure you're ready to see.

This isn't a "find yourself" journey wrapped in Pinterest quotes and retreat brochures. This is a homecoming. But not the kind where you walk in and everything smells like cookies. No — this is the kind of homecoming where the house is a bit musty, the light bulbs are flickering, and there's a locked door in the basement you've been too afraid to open.

And still — you open it.

Becoming real means reclaiming the parts of yourself that were never truly gone — just edited, hidden, or muted for survival. It's not a rebrand. It's not a makeover. It's a messy, awkward unpeeling of everything you thought you had to be, so that what's underneath can breathe again.

Remember *The Velveteen Rabbit*? That book with the stuffed animal who becomes real through love and wear and time? The rabbit doesn't become real by being the shiniest, the prettiest, the most functional. He becomes real through *use*. Through experience. Through being held and dropped and stitched back together. The same is true for you. Your Real Self isn't the perfect, polished version. It's the one that has scars, wrinkles, stories — and is still standing.

And if you're reading this, chances are your Real Self has been whispering for a while. Maybe not with words. Maybe through burnout. Or rage. Or apathy. Maybe through a numbness you can't shake. That's the thing about exile — the self you push away doesn't disappear. It just gets louder in different ways.

Sometimes it comes out sideways. In self-sabotage. In picking fights with people who love you. In overworking until you collapse. In abandoning hobbies that once lit you up because now they feel like one more thing to optimize. In eating the whole bag of chips because you've been starving — not for food, but for *freedom*.

Perfectionism is always lonely. It promises belonging, but only if you behave. It promises safety, but only if you shrink. And eventually, you start to wonder whether the acceptance you've earned is even real — or if people just like the version of you that never makes waves.

So what happens when you start making waves?

Just so you know… the world doesn't end.

Some people will drift. Some people will pout. Some people will double down on their expectations and try to guilt you back into the mold you've outgrown. But others — the ones worth keeping — will *lean in*. They'll breathe easier around you. They'll feel more allowed to be themselves. Your courage will give them permission.

That's what becoming real does. It doesn't just set you free. It ripples outward. It unshackles.

But this is where most people get stuck. They think becoming real requires a grand reinvention. That they need to move countries or quit jobs or shave their heads or write a dramatic Instagram post with the caption "New Era."

Nope. Becoming real isn't dramatic. It's deliberate.

It's saying no when you used to say yes.

It's letting the silence hang instead of filling it with a fake laugh.

It's telling your partner, "I'm scared," instead of pretending you're fine.

It's wearing the outfit that feels good instead of the one that looks 'appropriate.'

It's rediscovering the sound of your *own* voice — not the one that gets claps, likes, or nods of approval, but the one that feels like home in your throat.

And here's the wildest part: your nervous system is built for this.

You've probably trained it to associate authenticity with danger, especially if vulnerability wasn't safe in your childhood or if you've lived in high-pressure environments. But brains are plastic. They can rewire. They can learn that safety isn't in perfection — it's in congruence.

So how do you start?

Proven Tools to Reconnect With the Self You Exiled:

1. Parts Work / Internal Family Systems (IFS). Begin identifying the internal voices you've mistaken for "you." There's the Inner Critic. The Achiever. The Caretaker. The Rebel. Instead of silencing them, get curious. Ask: What is this part trying to protect? Behind every part is a younger self that formed out of necessity. Talk to them. Befriend them. Reassure them. That's how you earn your own trust.

2. The Empty Chair Technique (Gestalt Therapy). Sit across from an empty chair. Imagine your child self — the one before the performance — sitting in it. What do they need to hear? What are they afraid of? What did they want to become? Speak it aloud. This practice has been shown to improve emotional processing and self-compassion.

3. Creative Freewriting. Set a timer for 10 minutes and write whatever comes to mind using your non-dominant hand. It slows the brain down and bypasses the critical mind. Often, what shows up on that page sounds like the true voice beneath the persona. Let it.

4. Somatic Inquiry. Drop into the body. Where do you feel tension when you think of "being yourself"? Name it. Breathe into it. Movement-based therapies like yoga, TRE (tension and trauma releasing exercises), or dance are powerful here. Your body remembers who you are.

5. Dream Tending. Instead of interpreting your dreams literally, sit with the characters and images. What do they represent in you? Dreams are the subconscious speaking. Treat them with curiosity, not control.

6. Reconnection Ritual: The Inner Child Prompt Journal Ask yourself daily:

- What would little me have loved to do today?
- Where did I feel most like myself?
- What did I pretend to be okay with, but wasn't?

You don't need to answer perfectly. You just need to start listening.

So, now after you've heard your own voice like never before, you've cracked the door open. You've peeked behind the polished persona and glimpsed the part of you that's been tapping the glass this whole time, asking, "Hey, is it safe yet?" And here's the weird part: reconnecting with that self isn't always liberating. Sometimes, it's *gutting*.

Becoming real doesn't just mean rediscovering joy or curiosity or creativity. It also means grieving the years — maybe decades — you spent suppressing them. It means mourning all the times you said yes when you meant no. All the friendships you built on being agreeable. All the effort you poured into being lovable *instead of* being known.

And grief is sneaky. It doesn't just arrive with tears and sad music. Sometimes it shows up as anger. As restlessness. As that hollow feeling in your chest when you realize how long you've been performing, even for yourself. It's not self-pity. It's the ache of waking up.

The good news? That ache is a sign of life.

There's a phrase in psychology called **"cognitive dissonance"** — that uncomfortable tension between what you believe and how you behave. When you're becoming real, you'll feel it often. You'll say things that sound like the old you, while internally cringing because they no longer feel true. You'll notice how often you laugh when something's not funny, or apologize when you've done nothing wrong, or smile when you're actually seething.

This in-between space — where the Real You is emerging but hasn't yet taken the wheel — is the most uncomfortable and the most crucial. This is here where you build capacity by making micro-adjustments:

- You tell the truth, even if your voice shakes.

- You speak slower, so your body can keep up with your words.

- You sit with the silence after a boundary, instead of backtracking to make it softer.

- You stop trying to be relatable, and start being *real*.

And yes, people will notice.

Some will find it threatening. After all, your performance made *them* comfortable. They liked the easy version of you, the one who overdelivered and never made things awkward. But let them flinch. Let them misinterpret. That's not a sign you're doing it wrong — it's a sign you're no longer filtering your truth for mass consumption.

Others, though? They will lean in. Because realness is magnetic. It cuts through the noise. It makes space for the unspoken parts in everyone else. Your willingness to go first — to drop the mask — will show others they can do the same. Not by preaching. By embodying.

That's how cultural change starts. Not with slogans or manifestos. But with one person deciding they're done faking it. One person letting their voice shake, letting their laugh be too loud, letting their heart show up in the room *without* dressing it up as a TED Talk.

And that's where we'll leave this part of the journey.

With you. Here. In the glorious mess of rediscovery.

The next part of this book isn't about the past. It's about what you build from here. You've unearthed the raw material. Now it's time to shape it. To live from it. To stop being a rough draft of who you think you should be — and finally, write the real damn story.

So take a breath. You've earned it.

In Chapter 7, we'll explore what it means to create a life aligned with your Real Self — not as an aesthetic, but as a structure. A rhythm. A way of showing up daily that feeds, rather than hides, who you are.

See you on the other side.

YOU'RE THE REASON SOMEONE ELSE WILL FINALLY BREATHE OUT

If this book has already cracked something open for you... a thought, a pattern, a pressure you've carried for too long, then you're in a rare position:
you can make that same breakthrough possible for someone who hasn't found this book yet.

All it takes is a **30-second signal boost**.

Readers don't find books like this because an algorithm is generous.

They find them because **someone like you** left a trail.

A small review does two things:

1. **It tells someone out there that they aren't the only one fighting perfection.**

2. **It tells the system that this book is worth surfacing.**

If you're willing to be that person, the one who quietly helps strangers feel less alone, scan the QR code below and leave a quick, honest review.

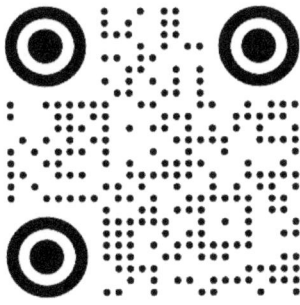

And if you want early access to new books, behind-the-scenes writing updates, and extra tools that don't make it into the published pages, you can join the mailing list.

You're not just reading a book.

You're shifting a culture that has demanded flawless performance for far too long.

Thanks for being one of the brave ones.

PART 3:

THE UNLEARNING

CHAPTER 7:

THE BRAVE DAY CHALLENGE

Your so-called flaws might be the most magnetic thing about you.

Seen and Still Standing: Stories of Radical Visibility

Most of us have a running list in our heads titled: "Things That Will Definitely Kill Me If Anyone Ever Finds Out." It might include the fact that you sometimes rehearse confrontations in the shower. Or that you once failed spectacularly at something everyone else found easy. Or maybe it's the jagged scar on your stomach, the awkward laugh you try to smooth over, or the way you speak too fast when you're nervous. These are the parts you work overtime to manage, edit, polish, or bury... because somewhere along the way, you were taught they made you unlovable. Unsafe. Unworthy.

Radical visibility is about dragging those parts into the light and saying, "Yup, this is me." Not as a performance. Not to be edgy. But because living with your full self, locked in the attic is no way to live at all.

And you know what? **Most people are desperate for someone else to go first.**

We spend so much of our lives trying to be palatable that we forget how magnetic the truth is. Realness cuts through the noise. Think about the last time someone told you something vulnerable and unpolished — maybe a friend who admitted they do a superman pose in the bathroom mirror before work, or a stranger on social media who shared a barefaced selfie with a caption about grief. You didn't recoil. You leaned in. You respected the hell out of it.

Let's talk about *real people who went first.*

Like the girl on TikTok with cystic acne who posted her face without makeup for 30 days straight. At first, the comments were brutal. Internet trolls did their internet troll thing. But by day 10, something shifted. People started thanking her. Sharing their own stories. One person wrote, "I showed my boyfriend my bare face for the first time in six months because of you." She wasn't a skincare guru. She wasn't trying to sell anything. She just got tired of hiding. And that rawness — that refusal to filter out her humanity — was more powerful than perfection ever could be.

Or take Hasan Minhaj, who talked openly in his comedy special about being racially profiled, family trauma, and the pressure to make his immigrant parents proud. He did it with humor, yes, but he also let the cracks show. He told a story about rejection — standing outside his crush's house on prom night, dressed up, waiting, only to find out she had already left with someone else. That moment, painful and raw, was the one audiences never forgot.

Or Lizzo, dancing in lingerie on Instagram, unapologetically taking up space as a plus-sized Black woman in a culture that tries to make people like her invisible. She isn't just a body-positive icon. She's a permission slip.

Visibility isn't about oversharing. It's about *undoing the shame* around being seen. It also doesn't mean you owe your story to everyone. It means you stop performing for a hypothetical audience in your head. You stop editing yourself down to fit a mold no one really likes anyway.

Of course, this isn't easy. Especially if you've spent decades perfecting the disguise. Especially if being too much, too loud, too weird, or too sensitive once cost you something.

But here's the good news: being seen doesn't have to start big. In fact, it shouldn't.

It can start by wearing something you love even if it's "not flattering." It can start by speaking up in a meeting, even if your voice shakes. It can start by posting the photo you like but usually delete. It can start by saying, "Actually, I don't agree," and letting the silence hang.

That's the thing about visibility — it's not a one-time event. It's a repeated risk, a practice of self-reclamation in real-time. And yes, sometimes it feels like walking into the arena naked with a target painted on your chest. But what if that very exposure — the part that feels like a curse — is what makes you irresistible?

Radical visibility doesn't mean being loud, extroverted, or constantly online. It means being **unapologetically congruent** — matching your insides with your outsides, even when it's inconvenient or weird or not especially flattering. It means telling your boss that a project's unrealistic instead of faking optimism and quietly panicking. It means saying "I'm not ready" or "I changed my mind" or "I'm not okay" and letting that land without apology.

It means admitting you hate yoga, even though your friends swear by it. It means being the only person not drinking at the work event and not inventing an excuse. It means refusing to retouch the zit in your photo because — shocker — you have a living face, not a mask.

The reason this kind of visibility feels radical is because we live in a world that rewards the opposite. Performance. Palatability. The illusion of perfection. Think about it: we have entire platforms built on curation. Dating apps with six-photo summaries of your entire being. Corporate job interviews where you're expected to pitch yourself like a startup. Visibility has been hijacked by branding. And we've forgotten how to just be.

When you choose radical visibility, you're not just showing yourself — you're rejecting a system that profits off your shame.

And you don't have to be famous or fearless to do it. Remember that woman on TikTok who stopped straightening her hair after 20 years and documented the awkward grow-out phase? Or the dad who started sharing videos of himself learning ballet at 47? Or the teenager with a stutter who began reading poetry on YouTube — pauses and all? Their reach wasn't in their polish. It was in their realness.

What made them powerful wasn't that they were the best. It's that they were brave *enough*. And every time they pressed publish or stepped into a room as themselves, they rewrote a narrative — not just for themselves, but for whoever was watching and wondering... *Hey, maybe I can do that too?*

This is where visibility becomes contagious. When you go first, you light a path. And while you may not hear it, someone... somewhere, is whispering "thank you" just because you existed out loud.

So what's your version of going first?

- Is it wearing shorts even though you hate your knees?
- Is it sharing your real opinion in a meeting, even if no one else agrees?
- Is it posting that poem, song, drawing, or confession that feels a little too raw?
- Is it saying, "This is me. I'm done editing."

Start there.

You don't need a viral moment. You need a private one — the kind that shifts something inside you, even if no one claps. Especially then.

In the next chapter, we'll move from watching others be visible to becoming visible ourselves — not just once, but as a conscious, daily choice to live unfiltered, unmasked, and unapologetically real… because the goal isn't to impress. It's to *inhabit*.

From Exposure to Embodiment

There's a reason visibility feels like standing naked on a stage with a spotlight in your face and a silent crowd watching. It's one thing to *want* to be seen. It's another thing entirely to **let yourself be seen** — unfiltered, unpracticed, in motion rather than in summary. And the moment after you finally hit "post," or say the unscripted truth, or show up not as a brand but as a breathing human… that moment can feel like free fall.

But here's the thing no one tells you: visibility isn't a single act. It's a practice. It's not the mic drop, it's the mic check, over and over. It's not about making a scene, it's about taking up your rightful place *in* the scene, without apologizing for the space you occupy.

And maybe you don't want to be an influencer or a keynote speaker or a memoirist airing every detail of your life. That's fine. Visibility doesn't require that you spill everything. It simply asks that you stop hiding the truth when it matters.

And yes, this will be terrifying if your body has learned that being visible equals being vulnerable, and being vulnerable equals danger. If you've ever been mocked, dismissed, punished, or exiled for showing your real self, then "just being yourself" doesn't feel like advice… it feels like a trap.

That's why we start small. Embodiment means **choosing to stand fully in your own skin** even when there's no audience, no camera, no applause. It means practicing authenticity as a verb, not a vibe.

It could look like walking into a room without shrinking your posture. It could mean asking the question no one else wants to ask. It could mean answering "How are you?" with something other than "Busy" or "Fine."

It could mean wearing something that actually feels like *you* — not the version you curate for work, for brunch, for safety.

There's a scene in *Fleabag* where a character says, "Hair is everything." And while it's hilarious, it also speaks to something deeper. The choices we make with our appearance, our voice, our energy — they *are* everything, not because they define our worth… no… they reflect our alignment.

You don't need to prove your worth through performance. But you *can* start practicing truth through embodiment. Through micro-moments of honesty. Through letting your real self leak out, even just a little, and watching what happens.

And you know what? The world won't collapse.

But here's what might: the stories you've told yourself about how you **must be in order to belong.**

And after you did the thing and let yourself be seen… I don't know what you've chosen. Maybe you posted the picture without the filter. Maybe you told the truth in a room full of people who are used to your agreeable nod. Maybe you wore the shirt that shows your arms, the ones you've spent years hiding under sleeves and shame. Whatever your version was, you stepped out. And it felt like a drop tower ride — the slow, shaky ascent, then that sudden lurch in your stomach as gravity yanked your insides to your ankles.

So how do you do that? How do you stay when your instinct is to flee?

You regulate. You don't bulldoze through the fear — you sit with it. You create micro-moments of congruence where your inside and outside match, and you let those moments stack.

Try this: next time you share something vulnerable, whether it's online or in a conversation, immediately follow it with a grounding ritual. Put your hand on your chest and name what you're feeling. Text a friend who gets it. Take a walk and remind your body that nothing bad is happening. That you're safe now. That you're allowed to be seen.

This is how you teach your system that truth isn't always punished. That boldness isn't always followed by exile.

And if you *do* experience pushback or judgment — because let's be honest, sometimes the world is still a shitshow — you give yourself context. You remind yourself that the criticism isn't proof you were wrong to speak. It's proof that your truth poked someone else's fear. That's not yours to carry.

Embodiment is also about consistency. Not performance — consistency. You don't need to bare your soul every day or shout your story from the rooftops. Sometimes embodiment looks like maintaining eye contact when you would've looked away. Sometimes it's ordering what you actually want, not what you think you *should*. Sometimes it's not deleting the post, not backtracking in the meeting, not apologizing for taking up space.

The goal isn't to be fearless, but to expand your window of tolerance for authenticity. To stretch it, gently. To let your nervous system catch up to your courage.

And here's the thing — your nervous system *can* catch up. Neuroplasticity is real. You can rewire the associations between visibility and danger. It takes time. It takes patience. But it's possible.

There will be days when you fall back into the old patterns — when you shrink, edit, people-please, ghost, but that doesn't mean you've failed. It means you're human. It means you're rewiring, and the old path still has grooves.

So you forgive yourself... And you try again.

You take one more step toward living in a way that matches who you *really* are — not just when it's easy, but when it's terrifying.

Not just in moments of exposure, but in the mundane, unglamorous dailiness of being.

That's embodiment.

That's the new brave.

And in the next chapter, we'll explore what to do when the fear *does* catch up to you — how to handle the inevitable shame whiplash that can follow vulnerability, and how to calm the internal storm without betraying your growth.

CHAPTER 8:

LETTING GO WITHOUT GIVING UP

You don't have to stop caring.
You just don't have to die for it.

C+ Work and the Radical Act of Rest

You've probably heard some version of the phrase "don't let perfect be the enemy of good." But perfectionism doesn't stop at making good feel not good enough — it makes *anything short of an A+ feel like failure*. B+? Lazy. C+? Might as well not have shown up. Rest? Irresponsible.

We're not talking about high standards here. We're talking about a system that equates worth with output, and output with excellence, and excellence with being constantly "on." And somewhere along the way, rest became synonymous with guilt. You might physically lie down, but inside your head? You're editing tomorrow's email while mentally calculating your caloric intake and flagellating yourself for not using your weekend to finally clean out that drawer. You know the one.

C+ work isn't laziness. It's rebellion. It's you saying, "I'm showing up as I am, not as I'm curated to be." It's trusting that your okay version is still valid. It's letting things be sufficient instead of impressive. And if you've been raised on gold stars, achievements, and the high of being exceptional, then turning in C+ work can feel like standing in public wearing socks and sandals. Exposed. Vulnerable. A little gross.

But here's the truth no one told us: your body, your relationships, your *life* can't run on A+ mode forever. It wasn't designed for it. You weren't designed for it. Perfectionism is a glitch in the nervous system that keeps you in performance mode even when the curtain's down. You start believing that if you just work a little harder, stretch a little thinner, stay a little longer, *then* you'll be allowed to rest.

You won't. The bar moves. Every time.

And the cost isn't just exhaustion. It's joy. It's creativity. It's presence. You stop noticing the way the light hits the table in the morning because you're too busy trying to clear the table. You stop dancing because there's no point if you're not good at it. You start associating "relaxation" with failure. And then you wonder why you're burned out, anxious, or dissociated.

So what if you let the laundry pile up a bit? What if your next meeting deck is *fine*, not phenomenal? What if you skipped the meal prep and had toast for dinner and no one fucking died?

There's a difference between not trying and *not contorting*. C+ work says: I care enough to show up — but not enough to lose myself in the process.

And look, I get it. If you're used to high achievement, to that addictive hit of being praised for overdelivering, then anything less feels like slacking. Mediocre is a dirty word. But mediocrity, when done consciously, can be healing. Strategic. Revolutionary.

Because when you finally stop equating your value with your performance, something wild happens: you rest. Not just physically. But mentally. Emotionally. Existentially. And from that place? You might just find the energy to create something truly meaningful.. just because it feels good.

But you won't get there by sprinting. You'll get there by laying down.

You'll get there by leaving the email draft half-finished and walking barefoot outside instead. You'll get there by choosing the early night over the extra edit. By letting the call go to voicemail. By saying, "Not today." You'll get there by resisting the itch to optimize every pocket of your damn day and finally realizing that healing often looks like *doing less* — and being okay with it.

Rest, real rest, isn't a reward. It's a requirement. And in a culture that worships hustle, choosing to rest is a radical act. It's a protest sign scrawled in nap ink that says: "I am not a machine."

But of course, you've probably heard all that before. You might've even nodded along while reading, half-convinced. The hard part isn't knowing rest is good for you — the hard part is *allowing* it. Especially when your nervous system still registers downtime as a threat. When silence makes your skin crawl. When stopping feels like failure.

So let's get practical.

Start by *scheduling* your C+ work. Literally — mark it in your calendar: "10:00–10:30: Do a half-assed job." Pick something small: an email reply you're overthinking, a meal you want to make "perfect," a workout you usually push through like a Navy SEAL. Now? Do it at 70%. Hell, do it at 40%. Then walk away. Do not go back. Do not tweak. Do not perfect.

Next: give your nervous system proof that rest is survivable.

Lie down in the middle of the day. Don't earn it. Don't disguise it as a "power nap." Just rest because you're a mammal, and mammals aren't meant to be productive 16 hours a day. At first, you'll feel itchy. Guilt will come crawling. Let it. Breathe through it. The goal isn't to be comfortable — it's to be congruent.

Then there's the storytelling part. And the chances are, your inner narrator still thinks rest is risky. That story was probably born when you were young — maybe you got praised for pushing through, maybe you got love for your results, maybe you learned that being "useful" was safer than being needy. So now you're going to write a new script.

Try this:

"I'm allowed to rest, even if nothing is finished. I'm allowed to rest, even if someone else is disappointed. I'm allowed to rest, because I exist — not because I earned it."

Say it. Write it. Make it your phone background. Tattoo it on your brain. As the only way out of perfectionism is *through* — and sometimes, through looks like crawling under a blanket and watching trash TV while your inner critic screams. Let it scream. You don't have to answer.

You're recovering.

And recovery is sacred. It's messy and slow and inconvenient and powerful. You're unhooking your identity from your output. You're letting your nervous system remember what stillness feels like. You're re-learning that you are allowed to exist without justifying it every second.

That's not giving up.

That's *coming home.*

Redefining Productivity, Progress, and "Success"

You know, this whole time we've been measuring success with the wrong ruler.

Somewhere along the way, "productive" stopped meaning *useful* or *meaningful* and started meaning *busy*. "Progress" got hijacked by the to-do list industrial complex. And "success"? Don't even get me started. It got Photoshopped, filtered, optimized, and turned into a performance — a lifestyle aesthetic more than a lived reality.

You want to know the truth?

You can be productive and still be empty.
You can make progress in all the wrong directions.
You can succeed and still feel like a failure inside your body.

Because if you never *redefine* what those words mean for you, you'll live your entire life chasing someone else's finish line — and when you get there, it won't feel like arriving. It'll feel like being late to a party that already moved on.

Let's talk about productivity first. Our culture worships it. Hustle is still being peddled like it's the answer to self-worth. Even when we *know* better — even when we've read the research, done the therapy, burned out three times and lived to limp through it — there's still this twitch in the brain that says, "What have you achieved today?" Like if we can't answer that with a tangible result or a gold star, we've somehow failed the day.

But productivity, in its truest form, isn't about output. It's about alignment. Did you do what mattered today? Did you act in a way that supports the life you actually want — not the one your fear is managing like a PR firm on crack?

And look, maybe what mattered today wasn't launching a side hustle or doing a juice cleanse. Maybe it was calling your grandma. Maybe it was deleting the app that's been making you feel like garbage. Maybe it was writing two messy sentences of the novel you're afraid will suck.

Maybe it was *not quitting* when your brain told you to.

That counts.

Now let's shift to "progress." Oh, sweet linear progress, how we have been misled. We've been sold this idea that progress is clean and linear, that it looks like a staircase you climb in increasingly impressive shoes. But real progress? It's weird. It loops. It doubles back. It involves days when you're curled on the floor wondering if anything's changing, and then one random Tuesday, you realize you didn't people-please in a meeting and suddenly you're crying in a parking lot because that's *actual* growth.

Progress isn't just about doing more or getting better. Sometimes it's about doing less and *not reacting*. Sometimes it's about not spiraling when you didn't get an immediate reply. Sometimes it's about pausing before saying yes. Sometimes it's just…not losing your shit over things that used to trigger you every time.

That is *wild* progress. But it's quiet. Invisible. And if you're not careful, you'll miss it — or worse, dismiss it — because it didn't come with applause.

Now, success. That slippery, shape-shifting beast.

Success is one of those concepts that looks stable until you start asking questions. Whose version of success are you actually chasing? Is it your parents'? Your ex's? The algorithm's? Your old boss who used to reward burnout with praise?

If your nervous system still thinks you're only lovable when you're impressive, then no matter how much you achieve, it will never be *enough*. You'll keep upping the bar like an Olympic coach with zero chill, and each time you land a goal, you'll feel nothing. Maybe even worse than nothing — maybe a weird existential anticlimax, like, "Is this it?"

So what if success didn't mean status, followers, weight loss, or external proof?

What if it meant *peace of mind*?
Or finally sleeping through the night without clenching your jaw?
Or being honest in a room where you used to shrink?
Or laughing — loud and ugly and free — without covering your mouth?

What if the most successful people weren't the ones who looked the best on paper, but the ones who felt most like themselves when no one was watching?

That version of success? It's quieter. But holy shit, is it potent.

And the best part? You don't have to climb some mythical mountain to find it. You don't have to bleed for it. You just have to stop outsourcing your definition to people who benefit from your confusion.

You just have to stop. Just long enough to ask: what does success *feel* like in your body?

Not what it looks like. Not what it earns. Not what other people will say. What does it *feel* like? Because if the answer is "tight," "numb," "pressure," or "never quite enough," then congratulations — you've just uncovered a borrowed definition.

Try this:

Exercise: Rewrite the Ruler

Grab a blank page (or your phone notes app if you're allergic to paper). Write the words:

"Success, for me, feels like…"
…and finish that sentence ten times.

Don't overthink it. Let it get weird. Let it be inconsistent. Let it contradict your LinkedIn bio. Example?

- Success, for me, feels like a day when I don't explain myself.

- Success, for me, feels like finishing work while the sun's still up.

- Success, for me, feels like eating a sandwich in silence, undistracted.

- Success, for me, feels like saying "No thanks" and not following it with a paragraph.

Next, write:
"Progress, for me, looks like…" — and again, ten endings.

- Progress, for me, looks like not checking my ex's socials.

- Progress, for me, looks like letting someone else lead the meeting.

- Progress, for me, looks like *not* fixing other people's moods.

- Progress, for me, looks like remembering to drink some damn water.

You'll start to notice something wild: none of these require medals, applause, or viral reels. They just require awareness. Choice. A little gentleness toward your brain, which has been conditioned for years to believe that productivity is the price of love, and success is the only currency of belonging.

It's not.

And here's a reframe that might blow the circuits in your perfectionist wiring:
You're allowed to be proud of things no one claps for.
You're allowed to count quiet healing. Half-efforts. Not losing your shit. You're allowed to celebrate *non-events* — like the fight you didn't start, the spiral you interrupted, the boundary you held.

Now, let's deal with the cult of hustle one last time, because that ideology dies hard.

The decline of traditional 9-to-5s didn't free people — it just shifted the burden. Everyone's an entrepreneur now. Everyone's "building something." Everyone's expected to monetize their passion, scale their purpose, become their own brand. And guess what? That pressure *also* comes with a dress code, a timeline, and a relentless undercurrent of performance.

Even rest got colonized.
Take a nap? Better document it for your "soft life era."
Declutter your closet? Make it aesthetic.
Drink water? Link the bottle, babe.
Self-care is now a micro-influencer genre with its own ambient playlist.

No wonder your brain is fried.
No wonder your body thinks it's never done enough.
You're not broken. You're *exhausted* from running in a race where the finish line is imaginary and the judges keep changing the rules.

So what do we do?

We opt out.

One conscious act at a time, we stop performing for the algorithm. We stop feeding the part of our psyche that needs to be seen as impressive to feel safe. And we start reclaiming the metrics that actually matter — the ones that whisper, not shout.

Things like:

- Am I aligned with what matters to me?

- Am I present in my own life?

- Am I treating my body like a teammate, not a mule?

- Am I proud of the way I move through the world — even when no one's looking?

Real success doesn't scream... It doesn't trend.
And it sure as hell doesn't require you to burn out just to prove you're worthy of rest.

Sometimes it just feels like quiet peace. Like not having to prove anything today. Like sitting in your own skin and thinking, "This'll do."

Sometimes, success sounds a lot like silence — the good kind.

And as we ease out of this chapter, into the next, that silence?
That's where the real magic starts.

Because now that we've challenged what the world told you to value, it's time to do the messy, wild, human thing next:

Let go without giving up.

We'll meet you there.

Do It Messy: Done Is Better Than Perfect

You know what kills more dreams than failure ever could? **Waiting until it's perfect.**

We've all done it — the endless tinkering, the obsessive planning, the 47 open browser tabs for "research." The belief that one day we'll feel ready, polished, fully formed, with glowing skin and zero self-doubt, and *then* we'll do the thing. We'll launch the website. Submit the pitch. Have the hard conversation. Start the goddamn painting.

Except that day never comes. Because perfection is not a milestone. It's a mirage.

And the longer you wait for everything to line up just right, the more likely it is that the thing never gets done. Not because you didn't care — but because you cared so much, it crushed you.

This is where "done is better than perfect" stops being a Pinterest quote and starts becoming a survival skill.

But doing it messy doesn't mean you don't give a shit. It means you're **choosing momentum over paralysis**. It means you're willing to be seen in-process, unfinished, flawed, real. And that's terrifying — especially if your identity has been built on applause, achievement, or never letting anyone see you sweat.

But real life? Real growth? It's sweaty. It's awkward. It includes stutters and backspaces and "oh god did I really say that?" moments.

It includes your voice cracking during the speech. The typo in your resume. The painting that turned out looking more like a crime scene than a landscape.

It includes pressing publish with shaky hands, sending the message even when you want to puke, launching something before you've over-researched it into the ground.

Perfectionism loves research. Loves preparation. Loves the illusion of control. It'll keep you in prep mode forever, whispering "Just a little longer…" until you're 78 and still revising your About Me page.

Here's the truth bomb that helped me crawl out of that trap: **The first version is supposed to suck.** Not just acceptable-level cringe — actual, gritty, "please never show this to anyone" suckage.

That's how it works.

Your favorite book had a shitty first draft. Your favorite artist threw out entire sketchbooks. Your favorite speaker once blacked out mid-sentence and made a joke about diarrhea just to fill the silence. (Okay, maybe that one was me.)

And yet, we only see the highlight reel. So we think our messy middle means we're not cut out for it. When really, the mess is the price of admission. The tax for creating anything worth a damn.

This chapter — this whole damn book — wasn't born out of perfect circumstances. Some parts were written with tears in my eyes. Others after three coffees, two energy drinks and no shower. One section? Fully drafted while hiding in a bathroom stall at work. (Don't ask.)

But it got done. Just by putting time into it. Daily. One messy page at a time

And sometimes that's all the world needs. Not your polish. Not your perfection. Just your presence. Just you, in motion. You, creating a path by walking it. You, handing over a thing that might be a little rough around the edges — but holy hell, it's *real*.

And that realness is the part where we pick up next. As this isn't just about doing the thing — it's about surviving the voice that tells you it wasn't good enough once you did.

It's about **how to live with the *after*.** The post-post button panic. The "why did I do that" echo. The shame spiral that shows up uninvited and whispers, "You shouldn't have tried."

And listen, that voice is not a proof that you did something wrong. It's a proof you did something *new*. That voice is just your nervous system short-circuiting because you dared to leave the cave of safety and actually *ship* something.

Doing it messy means you'll face that voice more often — but it also means you'll build immunity to it. You'll start to recognize its bullshit tone. You'll get better at hearing it and still choosing to show up. Not in spite of it, but *alongside* it.

Here's a trick: when that voice kicks in, don't argue. Don't reason with it. Just say, "Thanks for your input," like you're dismissing a middle manager with a Napoleon complex. And then go do something ordinary — make tea, clean the sink, walk around the block. Give your nervous system a minute to catch up with your bravery.

And bravery doesn't always feel like a battle cry. Sometimes it feels like throwing up and pressing send anyway.

Messy action might leave a trail of typos, awkward moments, and projects you'd rather not revisit. But it also leaves behind *evidence*. Proof that you tried. Proof that you didn't wait for permission, polish, or perfection.

And that evidence stacks. Each little imperfect attempt builds the internal muscle of momentum. And momentum, over time, becomes a quiet kind of confidence — not the "look at me!" kind, but the "I did this once, I can do it again" kind.

So next time you hesitate — whether it's starting the business, asking the question, showing up to that first class where you know no one — ask yourself: is this fear a sign I'm not ready, or is it just a symptom of stepping outside the lines?

Messy is where the breakthroughs live.

Messy is where your actual voice shows up, unfiltered and unpolished, maybe with some eyeliner smudged halfway down your cheek — but *damn* if it isn't magnetic.

Messy is human. And human is what we're here for.

So finish the sentence, even if you hate it.

Post the thing, even if your hand shakes.

Dance at the wedding, even if your rhythm is a disaster.

Launch the messy version. Say the clumsy truth. Paint the crooked line.

Let the world meet you *before* you're ready.

"Done" opens doors that "perfect" never will.

And with that, we tiptoe into Chapter 9 — where we stop philosophizing about the problem and start rewiring the damn thing. Not just in our thoughts, but in our *bodies*. You ready? Let's reprogram.

CHAPTER 9:

REWIRING THE PATTERN

Perfectionism isn't cured by logic,
it's rewired through practice.

Catch It, Name It, Reframe It

Before we can unhook from perfectionism, we have to know what it *actually looks like* in real time. Not in theory. Not in hindsight. But in the messy middle — when you just can't finish that stupid email and keep rewriting it for the 27th time, or you get all turned and twisted because of that stubborn hair strand that keeps sticking out today, or when you tell yourself you can't start the project until you've cleared your schedule and cleaned your house and fixed your posture and healed your childhood.

Perfectionism isn't just that high-achiever vibe we sometimes brag about in job interviews. It's a sneaky little shape-shifter that hides in plain sight. It shows up as procrastination, comparison, micromanaging, emotional shutdown, endless tweaking, and that frozen feeling you get when a blank page is staring back at you. It's the reflex to fix instead of feel. To please instead of pause. **To *do* instead of *be*.**

So how do you stop it?

You start by ***catching it in the act***. The first part of this process — catch it — is mindfulness without the spiritual performance anxiety. You don't need incense or a meditation app (unless you want them). You just need awareness. The skill of noticing when perfectionism rears its head.

And it can be subtle. You might catch it in your body first — the jaw tightening, the breath shortening, the heart rate rising when you're about to send a message that feels "too direct." Or maybe it hits you in your language: "I *should* be able to do this." "If I can't do it perfectly, I'm not going to do it at all." "What will they think?" These aren't just random thoughts — they're warning sirens.

Catching it means spotting these sirens in the wild. **No judgment. Just data.** You don't have to fix anything yet. You just name what's happening.

Which brings us to the second part: *name it.* Give the thought, the urge, or the spiral a label. Not in a clinical, sterile way, but in a human, slightly ridiculous way that helps defang it. "Ah yes, here comes Perfectionist Patty again, convinced I need a thesis statement to send a Slack message." Or: "Oh look, it's my inner overachiever having a meltdown because I made a typo." You can even give your inner perfectionist a voice — maybe she sounds like a passive-aggressive aunt or a deranged life coach who drank too much kombucha and is being grumpy and gassed up.

The point is: **you name it to tame it.** When you call something out, you create distance from it. Suddenly, it's not *you* — it's a pattern. And patterns can be changed.

This is where the third part kicks in: *reframe it.* And no, I don't mean toxic positivity or plastering "I love myself" affirmations over your genuine struggle. Reframing isn't denial. It's choosing a new lens. A lens that sees progress instead of perfection. That sees showing up, even shakily, as success. That understands that effort is still effort even when the outcome isn't shiny.

Say you're avoiding a creative project because it feels too big and you're afraid you'll mess it up. Instead of letting that fear dictate your actions, you catch it — "I'm spiraling because I think this has to be flawless" — name it — "Classic perfectionist freeze response" — and reframe it — "What if I just wrote a crappy first draft and trusted I can improve it later?"

This process isn't just a mental trick. It actually rewires your brain. Neuroscience tells us that when we interrupt old thought loops and intentionally choose new ones, we're engaging neuroplasticity — the brain's ability to form new connections. Each time you catch, name, and reframe, you're strengthening a pathway that says: I can respond differently. I am not my fear. I am not my conditioning. I get to choose a new way.

And the more often you do it, the faster it becomes second nature. It won't always be graceful. Sometimes you'll catch yourself mid-shame spiral and go, "Goddammit, I'm doing the thing again," and that counts. That's the work. That *is* healing. Not perfection. Not clean, curated, filtered healing. But muddy, fumbling, real healing.

So, what do you do after you've caught the thought? Named it. Reframed it. What now?

You do it again. And again. And again. B because perfectionism is a sneaky bastard that doesn't evaporate the first time you outsmart it. It's wired into years — sometimes decades — of conditioning. Every time you respond differently, even a little, you're laying new neurological track. You're making the unfamiliar path feel more walkable.

But here's where people often get tripped up: they expect the new mindset to *feel* good right away. It doesn't. It feels wrong. Awkward. Like walking in shoes that almost fit but rub in weird places. That's because your nervous system has learned to associate anxiety with productivity, control with safety, performance with love. So when you stop feeding those loops, your brain doesn't throw a parade. It panics.

You might find yourself itching to go back. To polish the project one more time. To cancel the post. To apologize for something that didn't actually hurt anyone. That's normal. That discomfort isn't proof that you're doing it wrong — it's proof that you're doing something *new*.

Reframing isn't about being bulletproof, it's about staying in the moment long enough to not abandon yourself.

Let's ground this in an example. Say you're in a meeting and someone praises a colleague for their presentation. Your stomach drops. Your mind spins: *Why didn't they praise mine? Was mine not good enough? Should I have added that graph after all? Maybe I talk too much. Maybe I don't talk enough.*

Step one: **Catch it** — "Whoa, I'm spiraling into comparison and self-doubt."

Step two: **Name it** — "Classic perfectionism panic triggered by external validation."

Step three: **Reframe it** — "Their praise isn't my failure. My value doesn't change based on one meeting. I showed up. I contributed. That's enough."

You won't always believe the reframe at first. That's okay. Say it anyway. Think of it like updating your software. At first it glitches. Then it stabilizes. Then it runs smoother.

If this feels too abstract, here's a more tactical approach — a little cheat sheet you can use when the spiral kicks in:

The Reframe Quick Guide

- Instead of: *"If I don't do it perfectly, I shouldn't do it at all."*
  Try: *"Progress counts. Imperfect action is still forward motion."*

- Instead of: *"They're going to think I'm stupid if I mess this up."*
  Try: *"Everyone makes mistakes. Most people are too focused on themselves to notice."*

- Instead of: *"I have to do this myself or it won't be done right."*
  Try: *"Done is better than perfect. Shared responsibility isn't failure — it's sustainability."*

- Instead of: *"I should be further along by now."*
  Try: *"I'm growing at the pace I'm able to. That's valid."*

Start slow. One reframe a day. One spiral intercepted. That's it. You don't need to gut-renovate your brain overnight. Just start pulling the thread.

Mini Exercise: The Spiral Interruption Log

For one week, keep a tiny log on your phone or in a notebook. Every time you catch yourself spiraling, jot down:

1. **The trigger** (what set you off)

2. **The perfectionist thought** (what it said)

3. **Your reframe** (what you chose to say instead)

You don't need to be poetic. Just honest. At the end of the week, read them all. You'll notice patterns — the same few fears recycling themselves, wearing different hats. You'll also see proof that you're building muscle.

And as that muscle grows, you'll feel it — the shift from reactive to responsive. From auto-pilot to agency. From shame to self-trust.

It's not a clean arc. Some days you'll kill it. Other days you'll spiral six times before lunch. Doesn't matter. Every time you choose awareness over autopilot, you win. And every win rewires something, even if you can't see it yet.

Regulate, Don't Perform (Somatic Tools & Nervous System Resets)

Most of us are so used to *performing* regulation that we don't even know we're doing it. We've picked up all the right scripts, the trendy buzzwords, the body scans and breathing exercises we half-remember from that podcast with the soothing voice. We *know* the right answers — we just don't feel any fucking better.

That's because perfectionism doesn't just make you hustle in your work or obsess over your appearance. It seeps into your healing, too. It convinces you that even your self-soothing must be impressive. That your nervous system must be "regulated" in a way that's visible, admirable, polished. You don't just cry — you have a cathartic release. You don't just rest — you take a photo of your tea, your journal, and your weighted blanket and call it #selfcare.

Regulation, when co-opted by perfectionism, becomes another performance. And instead of actually calming your system, you end up spiraling over whether you're doing it *right*. "Why am I still anxious if I meditated? Why do I still feel numb if I journaled?" And then comes the shame spiral: "I must be broken."

You're not broken. **You're just trying to *perfect* what can only be *felt*.**

Real regulation is inconvenient. It doesn't always look like peaceful yoga breathing in a clean, candlelit room. Sometimes, it looks like stomping your feet in your kitchen while blasting angry music. Sometimes it looks like curling up in bed and staring at the ceiling until your body softens on its own. Sometimes it looks like screaming into a pillow, or jumping in a cold shower, or whispering, "I'm safe" while your chest tightens and your hands tremble.

And sometimes, real regulation means *not* regulating right away. It means letting the wave crest instead of shutting it down. Because when your body is in survival mode — triggered, tense, hypervigilant — it's not asking for a technique. It's asking for *permission*. To feel. To move. **To exist without judgment.**

The body doesn't speak in logic or Instagram captions. It speaks in shivers, clenched jaws, racing hearts, stomach knots, heat, stillness. And if you listen closely — really listen — it will tell you exactly what it needs. But only if you're willing to stop performing and start responding.

We're conditioned to believe that a "regulated person" is someone who looks calm. But stillness is not always safety. Quiet is not always peace. Sometimes the most regulated person in the room is the one who's dancing like a maniac, or laughing too loud, or shaking out their limbs in the hallway between meetings. They're not trying to be chill. They're trying to be *free*.

And that's the pivot we need. **From trying to be palatable to trying to be present.**

Most perfectionists are walking around like tightly coiled springs in expensive shoes. They're over-functioning through their trauma, outpacing their own nervous systems, and then wondering why they snap at their partner, cry when the printer jams, or melt into a puddle of goo at the end of the week. It's not a moral failing. It's dysregulation.

You can read every book on mindset. You can affirm until your throat is sore. But if your body still thinks you're in a war zone, no amount of cognitive reframing is going to work. The body always votes last. And if your nervous system hasn't bought in, you're going to find yourself in the same pattern again and again: performing calm while clenching your jaw, smiling while your stomach flips, pushing through the day while your back screams for mercy.

Regulation is a physical recalibration of your threat response. And the fastest way to access that reset? Through the body. Not the brain.

Your nervous system has two main settings: fight/flight and rest/digest. Most perfectionists get stuck in the first one. Even when they're "relaxing," they're scanning for danger: emails, unreturned texts, a weird tone from their boss. Their foot never fully comes off the gas. And after a while, the brake lines just stop working.

This is where somatic tools come in. They aren't about fixing you. They're about *tuning in*. Think of it like running a software update on your body so your system can actually catch up to the reality that you're not being chased by a bear.

Let's try a few. Right now, wherever you are:

- Drop your shoulders. Seriously. Un-hunch them.
- Unclench your jaw. Your teeth aren't holding up the roof.
- Wiggle your toes.
- Exhale longer than you inhale. Count it: in for 4, out for 6.

- Press your feet into the floor like you're trying to leave a footprint.

These aren't cute little hacks. They're doorways. They signal to your body that it's safe enough to *not* be amazing for a second. **They interrupt the loop that tells you your worth is conditional.** They build a kind of embodied safety that no gold star ever could.

And when you start layering these into your day — not just during a meltdown, but *before* the moment of collapse — your baseline starts to change. You stop living on the edge of an emotional cliff. You stop needing to rehearse every conversation ten times. You stop barking at your partner for breathing too loud while being secretly afraid you're not enough.

You don't need to become a yogi. You don't need to meditate on a mountain. But you *do* need to come back into your body — the one you've probably spent years ignoring unless it was producing, performing, or looking socially acceptable.

Your body isn't an obstacle to perfection. It's the proof that you never needed to be perfect in the first place. It was never the right battlefield.

You're allowed to get quiet. To shake. To breathe. To slow down long enough to feel the things you've been skipping past for years. Regulation doesn't mean you won't still have ambition. It means your ambition won't be powered by panic.

This world doesn't need more high-achieving, emotionally constipated martyrs. What it really needs is people who can stay in their body while telling the truth. People who can hold space without collapsing. People who can breathe through the silence instead of filling it with apology.

You don't need to prove your peace. You just need to feel it.

And if you want to? You can start right now.

The Courage Comedown: Remedies for After You've Been Brave

So, you did the hard thing. You told the truth. Set the boundary. Showed your face. Shared the work. Laid yourself bare in front of people who could reject you, misunderstand you, or worse — ignore you entirely.

At first, it feels electric. You feel proud. Maybe shaky, but solid. Empowered even. You walk away thinking, *I did it. I was real. That was brave.*

And then... comes the comedown.

That awful, vulnerable hangover that hits a few hours or days later — when you start second-guessing everything you said, everything you did, every tiny facial twitch or weird laugh or slightly-too-loud opinion. It creeps in like fog: *Was that too much? Did I overshare? Do they hate me now?*

This is the Courage Comedown. It covers you after you stepped outside your carefully controlled performance mode, and now your nervous system is trying to recalibrate after being cracked open in public.

What's wild is that this isn't just psychological — it's physiological. Research on vulnerability shows that the brain registers social exposure much like it registers physical danger. The amygdala lights up. Cortisol spikes. Your body, bless it, can't tell the difference between being chased by a bear and being emotionally exposed on a podcast, a date, or in the middle of a team meeting.

And so it tries to protect you the only way it knows how: by flooding you with doubt and self-surveillance. By convincing you that next time, you should keep your mouth shut. Play it safe. Be likable. Be neutral.

This is why so many of us backpedal after a bold move. Why we soften our edges and apologize for our strength. Why we follow up with cringe texts or re-explain ourselves to people who probably weren't even thinking about it anymore. We're not actually responding to the world — we're responding to the *aftershock*.

That aftershock can be subtle, like a creeping unease, or loud, like full-body regret. Either way, it's a sign that your nervous system needs tending — not more convincing, not more logic, not a spreadsheet of "reasons why I'm allowed to be visible."

This is where most self-help advice fails. It teaches you how to *be* brave, but not how to *recover* from it. Visibility isn't a one-and-done thing. It's an emotional high-wire act. And what you do after the leap matters just as much as the leap itself.

And no, you're not weak for needing recovery. You're human. Even athletes don't sprint back-to-back without rest. Visibility, like any act of exertion, requires a cool down.

So if you're currently in the pit — replaying every word, feeling raw and overexposed — know this: it doesn't mean you shouldn't have said the thing. It means you're detoxing from the myth that you must always be perfectly composed to be worthy of being seen.

You're not unraveling. You're recalibrating.

So what helps? Pretending it didn't happen? Hustling to fix it? Hell no! What helps is creating a gentle landing for yourself, as intentional as the brave act that got you here. Below are some remedies — not rigid rules — to soothe the nervous system, regulate your self-concept, and keep you from crawling back into the bunker of self-erasure.

1. *Pre-decide your safe landing space.*

If you know you're doing something vulnerable — posting that honest reel, giving a talk, having the hard conversation — plan for the comedown ahead of time. Set up a calm evening. A walk. A playlist. A person you trust who won't try to fix you. Courage takes planning. So does self-kindness.

2. *Don't ask insecure people to validate your brave moment.*

You know exactly who I'm talking about. The friend who'll say "well maybe that was a bit much," or "I could never do that" — not out of concern, but out of projection. Choose your confidants wisely. Not everyone deserves access to your raw edges.

3. *Name the comedown for what it is — not a sign you messed up, but a sign your brain is detoxing fear.*

When shame creeps in, narrate it out loud: *"This is my nervous system trying to keep me safe. It thinks visibility is a threat. But I'm not in danger. I'm just uncomfortable."* That's not just woo-woo; that's neuroscience. Labeling emotions helps the brain shift from reaction to regulation.

4. *Avoid over-explaining.*

Do not send the triple text. Do not re-post with clarifications. Do not message your ex's new girlfriend to clarify what you meant by that Instagram caption. You're not actually clearing things up — you're trying to pull shame out of your body by controlling perception. That never works. Instead: breathe. Delete drafts. Let people think what they think.

5. *Meet yourself how you wish the world would.*

If you want applause, give yourself some. Literally. Clap. If you wish someone would say, "Wow, that was bold," say it to yourself in the mirror. Louder than feels natural. More dramatically than seems necessary. This isn't cringey. It's neural reinforcement.

6. *Do something grounding in your body.*

Stretch. Shake. Walk barefoot. Touch something cold. Visibility dysregulates not just the mind, but the body. You need to *move through it*, not just think your way out. Otherwise you stay trapped in the loop of mental panic — frozen in performance review mode.

7. *Make space for the comedown without making it your home.*

There's a difference between acknowledging discomfort and obsessing over it. Give it a timeframe. *"I get 24 hours to feel weird and raw, then I come up for air."* Set a timer. Light a candle. Ritualize it. Give it ceremony. Then, close the loop.

Because here's what's true: no one is thinking about your brave moment as much as you are. Most people are too wrapped up in their own post-performance panic to be dissecting yours. What you see as glaring — that joke that didn't land, the voice crack, the awkward pause — barely registers for anyone else.

So if today you're nursing the ache that comes after being bold — if your chest is tight and your brain's doing rewinds — here's your reminder: you were never supposed to be perfect. Just alive. Just honest. Just here.

That's what courage looks like on the other side. Messy. Tender. Shaky. But still standing.

And if you need to sit for a while before the next brave thing? Good. Pull up a chair. That's not backtracking — that's integration.

You've peeled back the layers. Named the pattern. Caught it mid-performance. Faced the sting of visibility and survived the comedown.

And maybe for the first time, you're realizing that healing isn't about becoming someone new — it's about *unbecoming* the version of you that was built to please, to perform, to stay small and polished and palatable.

Part IV is where we stop asking, *"How can I fix this?"* and start asking, *"What do I get to let go of?"*

You've done the hard part: staying awake.

Now let's get loud. Let's get messy. Let's unbecome everything you were never meant to be.

What to Do When You Slip Back

So, you've done all the work. You've named your patterns, regulated your nervous system, rewritten the inner script, and maybe even danced around the kitchen with the reckless joy of someone who just deleted their productivity tracker. And then — BAM — you wake up one day knee-deep in color-coded to-do lists, arguing with your partner about dishwasher stacking protocols like it's a UN peace negotiation, and obsessively editing a Slack message to make sure it doesn't come off "too much."

Welcome back. You slipped.

Now what?

Here's what most of us do: spiral. We spiral into shame, into panic, into that internal monologue that goes, *"I thought I was over this. Why am I like this? I'm a fraud. I've learned nothing."* It's like emotional whiplash, and the only logical response your brain can think of is to go harder. More rules, more self-monitoring, more pressure to get it right this time. It's the psychological equivalent of spilling a glass of wine and cleaning it with gasoline.

But what if we reframed the whole thing? What if slipping back wasn't a crisis, but a checkpoint? Like your brain's way of saying, *"Hey, just checking — are we really doing things differently now?"*

Because here's the truth: regression isn't failure. It's data. Your brain is testing the new system. Your body is adjusting to a different rhythm. You're navigating an entirely new way of being in the world — one that doesn't rely on old defaults. And that takes time. It takes muscle memory. It takes *reps*.

Think of it like this: if you've been walking in high heels for twenty years and suddenly switch to barefoot, you're going to wobble. You might even fall. That doesn't mean the heels were better. It just means your feet are relearning how to move like they were meant to.

Slipping back into perfectionist patterns isn't proof that you're broken — it's proof that you're in transition. And transitions are messy. They're also a goldmine of insight if you can stay curious instead of self-condemning.

So here's your job when you notice the slide:

1. **Name It Without Drama** — Don't turn it into a personality diagnosis. You didn't "ruin everything." You slipped. Say it out loud: *"Ah, look. There's my old pattern again."* Like you're spotting a raccoon in your backyard. Curious. Mildly amused. Slightly annoyed.

2. **Pause the Auto-Pilot** — Before you launch into 43 corrective behaviors, stop. Literally. Go for a walk. Touch something soft. Sit in a chair like you have nowhere to be. Interrupt the urgency loop.

3. **Check for Triggers** — What happened just before the backslide? Did someone give you vague feedback at work? Did your mom comment on your weight? Did you spend 45 minutes on Instagram and forget who you are?

4. **Choose a Micro-Reset** — You don't need to overhaul your life. You need a tiny re-anchor. Close the laptop early. Leave the email draft in drafts. Make boxed mac and cheese for dinner and eat it like a queen.

5. **Laugh. Seriously.** — Perfectionism is not funny. But how it tries to sneak back in? Hilarious. You, deep in analysis paralysis because you can't pick a font for your resume, as if Times New Roman holds the key to your destiny? Comedy gold.

There's something deeply healing about finding the absurdity in your own patterns. It breaks the spell. It gives you breathing room. It reminds you that this is all just a ride.

And finally, remember: no one heals in a straight line. Healing is a squiggly, loop-de-loop mess that often looks like regression from the outside. But on the inside, if you zoom in? Growth is happening. You're noticing faster. Recovering quicker. Forgiving more easily. That's progress.

Next time you slip, don't collapse into shame. Sit up. Look around. Dust yourself off. And with a wink and a smirk, say: *"Nice try, old programming. But I've got new moves now."*

So you've caught yourself in the act — chasing gold stars, agonizing over your "brand," folding laundry with the desperation of someone trying to win an Olympic medal in domesticity. Good. Not because you slipped, but because you *noticed*.

That moment of noticing? That's the win.

The goal was never to become some Zen cucumber who never reacts, never performs, never gets triggered by a well-placed humblebrag on Instagram. The goal is to catch it quicker. So you can reroute. Rewire. Rechoose. Again. And again.

This is what rewiring looks like. Not a light switch, but a thousand tiny dimmers. You turn them up, they flicker, sometimes they short-circuit, but you keep adjusting. Until one day you realize: wow, I don't even care that much about what Debra from HR thinks of my presentation font. Progress.

So what now?

1. Drop the Shame Rope

Shame is the hook that keeps you in the cycle. You slip, you feel bad, and to make yourself feel better… you reach for something performative. Something perfect-looking. And now you're back where you started, caught in a loop tighter than your old skinny jeans. The first step is to unhook. Say it out loud if you need to:

"I'm not bad. I'm just… in the middle of the process."

2. Zoom Out

If you catch yourself spiraling into microscopic self-loathing over how you spoke in that meeting, or how you parented today, or how you looked at that party, zoom out. Like, *Google Earth* levels of zoom. Ask yourself:

- Did anyone die?
- Am I catastrophizing?
- Would I care about this if I were on holiday with no phone?

3. Pick a Micro-Reset

You don't need a full 10-day silent retreat to reset. (Though if you do, good luck surviving the first 36 hours without coffee or talking.)

You just need one moment that reminds your nervous system: *we're safe now*. That could be:

- A walk without your phone
- A snack that has protein *and* joy (like cheese... with more cheese)
- Five deep breaths while whispering "you're not a productivity machine, you're a mammal"

These are not spiritual hacks. They are reminders that you are human, and that presence is an option available to you, even in this moment.

4. Set a Future Trap

If you know your triggers — like checking your inbox after 10 p.m. or doom-scrolling before bed — leave a note for future you. Literally. Sticky note. Phone wallpaper. Calendar alert titled "PUT IT DOWN." Whatever works. Don't rely on discipline. Rely on design.

5. Remember the Truth

Slip-ups aren't proof you're not growing. They're proof that growth is happening. You don't get to be great at this yet. You get to suck at it for a while. Grace means letting your nervous system have a say. It's going to flinch. It's going to overreact. It's going to default back to what it knows. That doesn't mean it failed you. It means it's trying to protect you with outdated software.

Update it with love, not shame.

And finally, remember this: the bravest people aren't the ones who never fall. They're the ones who fall and choose to get up *slower*. Softer. Smarter.

Next time you slip, don't collapse into shame. Sit up. Look around. Dust yourself off. And with a wink and a smirk, say: *"Nice try, old programming. But I've got new moves now."*

And speaking of new moves…

If Part III was about unlearning the performance script — the need to prove, impress, contort — then what comes next is something even scarier: learning how to *just be*. Without applause. Without overexplaining. Without trying to fix everything or everyone.

Part IV isn't about reaching a final form. It's about meeting yourself without the costume. Holding still long enough to hear your own voice again. Building a life that doesn't require constant upgrades. You ready?

Let's go find out what it actually means to live.

PART 4:

FREEDOM

CHAPTER 10:

YOU'RE THE JUDGE NOW

*No one is coming to save you,
and no one can stop you either.*

Digital Detox & the Trap of Self-Optimization

You wake up. You stretch. You reach for your phone. Before your feet hit the floor, you've already seen three people who worked out, two who launched businesses, one who made homemade oat milk, and a 19-year-old who just bought a house. You haven't even peed yet.

Welcome to modern life — where the internet isn't just a place to scroll, it's a coliseum of curated perfection. And even when we *know* it's a highlight reel, our brains don't. They see data. Repetition. Evidence. Proof that we're falling behind.

The perfectionism of the past wore a business suit and a polite smile. Today, it's wearing Lululemon, posting morning routines, and tracking "mental health days" on a Notion template. It's selling you a version of wellness so tightly wrapped in hustle energy that burnout becomes the aesthetic.

And it's not just Instagram. It's all of it — the endless productivity apps, biohacking podcasts, AI-enhanced calendars, and digital trackers that quantify how "well" you're sleeping, eating, moving, and meditating. Your nervous system is now part of an unpaid beta test.

We've replaced old-school achievement with a shinier model: *self-optimization*. But the promise is the same. If you just follow the right system, you'll finally be okay. Peace is now packaged as progress. And the to-do list? It's endless. Take supplements. Cold plunge. Journal. Time-block. Don't doomscroll. Connect with nature. Heal your inner child. Hydrate. Track macros. Meditate. Manifest. Monitor screen time. And whatever you do… don't fuck it up.

No wonder we're fried.

The irony? Most of these tools were designed to help. And for a while, some of them might. Until they don't. Until the tools become tasks, and your morning routine feels like a part-time job. Until your meditation app tells you you're on a 27-day streak, and now you're meditating *just to keep the streak alive*, not because you need to breathe. Until your "detox" becomes just another metric to optimize.

This isn't peace. It's perfectionism with better branding.

And the body — that inconvenient, intuitive, utterly honest companion — starts to whisper. Then shout. It tenses. It panics. It zones out. It can't keep up with the relentless pace of pretending to be well while secretly falling apart.

But here's the good news: you can walk away. You can put the phone down. You can decide that your worth isn't a graph. You can delete the app, ignore the trend, skip the reel, and let yourself be a soft, slow, gloriously inefficient human being.

And when you do, something wild starts to happen……

….you remember what your own voice sounds like.

Not the one that's rehearsed for Instagram captions or carefully modulated for Zoom calls. The real one. The one that hums under the surface when the world stops yelling for a second. That voice doesn't care about streaks. It doesn't need a 90-day plan. It just wants you to look up.

Because once the noise dies down, you notice that peace doesn't perform. It doesn't ask to be posted. It lives in the small, boring moments that don't make content — the dog hair on your socks, the weird bird you always forget the name of, the way the afternoon light hits your kitchen wall like a painting.

But those moments are fragile. They don't compete well with dopamine. The second you reintroduce the scroll — boom — the quiet is gone. You're back in someone else's rhythm, measuring yourself against someone else's morning. That's the trap.

And it's not that tech is evil or that you need to live off-grid and churn your own butter. It's just that perfectionism thrives in comparison — and comparison needs an audience. When you stop broadcasting and consuming constantly, the urgency softens. The pressure fades. You begin to want different things.

So how do you detox without swinging into full digital nihilism or smug superiority? You start by making peace boring again. You romanticize under-stimulation. You take the phone to another room — not because it's evil, but because you want to remember what your hands do when they're not curled around a rectangle of anxiety.

You also stop optimizing your healing. You don't track how long you went without checking email. You don't need a productivity tool to measure your rest. You rest. You log out. You breathe. You feel a little twitchy. Then you keep going.

Try a weekend without content. Try leaving your phone at home for a walk. Try existing without documenting it. You might find yourself noticing things again. You might get bored — and then curious. You might daydream. You might remember who you were before your life needed proof.

And if you fall off the wagon and binge on eight hours of TikTok, cool. That's not failure. That's feedback. Your brain was tired. You needed escape. Now you know. Now you choose again.

We're not going for perfection here — obviously. We're going for rewilding. For tuning back into your own cycles instead of obeying the endless algorithmic nudge that says you should be improving, even in your downtime.

You are not a startup. You're not a brand. You don't need to be optimized.

You're a person.

And people don't need dashboards.

They need rest.

They need awe.

They need enough stillness to remember what they actually want — not what they're being sold.

So go ahead. Log out. Shut it down. Take your nervous system off the grid.

You won't disappear.

You'll finally arrive.

You Get to Decide What Counts

There's a moment — maybe after the tenth burnout cycle, or maybe while staring blankly at a spreadsheet wondering how this became your life — when something in you quietly mutinies. A subtle but undeniable shift: *Wait... why am I still doing this? And who exactly am I doing it for?*

This is where the perfectionist script starts to fray. The one that told you achievement equals worth, productivity equals purpose, and suffering somehow proves you deserve a seat at the table. It doesn't unravel all at once. But the thread's been pulled.

You might find yourself skipping a meeting that could've been an email. Not answering a text right away. Choosing the slightly bruised banana because — gasp — it still tastes fine. And in those tiny acts of defiance, you start to realize: *You get to decide what counts now.*

That's not some fluffy Instagram quote. It's a fundamental rewiring of your internal GPS. Because for years (decades, maybe), you let other people's metrics measure your life: grades, likes, income brackets, thigh gaps, job titles, follower counts, how well you juggle ten flaming swords while smiling politely.

But those metrics were built for mass compliance, not personal fulfillment. They were designed to keep you busy proving yourself so you wouldn't notice how much of yourself you lost along the way.

So what *does* count?

That's the real question.

For some, it's the softness in their kid's laugh. For others, it's uninterrupted solo walks. A project that lights them up even if it never goes viral. A slow weekend. A fully-alive Tuesday.

You don't owe the world constant excellence. You don't owe your inner critic a damn explanation. You get to decide that cooking dinner counts. That canceling plans to sit in silence counts. That waking up without dread is a success metric. That not yelling when you wanted to *absolutely scream into the abyss* is progress.

And yeah, that means some people won't get it. Some will still be sprinting toward validation, convinced the gold stars mean something permanent. That's fine. Let them run. You've done your time in the race. And frankly, the trophy was cardboard.

Redefining what counts is pure leadership, as it is. The inward, cellular, *I-know-who-I-am* kind. It's reclaiming authorship over a life that was being ghostwritten by a system that never had your joy in mind.

And if your nervous system panics at the idea of setting your own standards, good. That means you're alive. It means you've been trained to outsource approval for so long that coming home to yourself feels… suspicious. Illicit, even. Like you're getting away with something.

You are. You're getting away with peace.

And the people who truly love you… the ones who see you beyond what you produce or prove? They'll adjust. Others will leave. Either way, your clarity will remain.

You can be excellent. You can strive, grow, achieve. But not from a place of lack. Not because your worth is on trial. Not because you're terrified of disappearing without your armor of accomplishment.

You decide what counts. And you decide it quietly, again and again, in the way you spend your time, your attention, your breath. In the things you water. In the things you let wither.

That's what liberation looks like… it looks like a mismatched outfit and a peaceful morning… it looks like finally deleting the LinkedIn app and not combusting… or it looks like unironically enjoying a mediocre sandwich without reviewing your life choices mid-bite…

It looks like letting yourself off the damn hook.

This is a revolution of scale — microscopic and seismic at once. You're building a life that makes *sense to you*. One where the metrics aren't weaponized. One where your value isn't measured in unread emails or how many back-to-back things you crushed today while smiling through the existential rot.

The culture won't reward you for this. It thrives on your discontent. It sells you fix-it plans and optimization apps and little dopamine pellets disguised as achievement. It keeps you chasing so you don't pause long enough to ask, "Hold on a minute… do I even want this?"

But you've paused now. You're asking. That means the spell is broken.

And sure, your nervous system might still throw a tantrum. You might wake up on Tuesday panicking that your to-do list doesn't justify your existence. You might feel weirdly guilty for resting on a Sunday without folding laundry, meal prepping, or doing something that can be hashtagged as #intentional. But that's just old wiring having a flare-up. Let it flare. Then go make yourself a snack and sit down anyway.

You're not becoming a slacker. You're becoming a sovereign.

Because once you learn that your worth was never up for debate, you stop trying to earn what was already yours. You stop asking perfection to promise you safety. You stop outsourcing your compass.

And what happens next?

You breathe. Like you've returned to your body after years of white-knuckling through the performance of a life that looked shiny but felt hollow.

You notice small things. Light on the wall. A funny-shaped carrot that looks a bit indecent (hello, Uncle Freud). A moment of stillness where your jaw isn't clenched and you feel a little bit liquid. That counts.

You start trusting yourself again — your no, your yes, your timing, your taste. You stop apologizing for the way your intuition whispers, "That's not for me," even when the world says, "But it should be."

And then, without fanfare, something wild happens: You become more *you*. Not the curated version. Not the high-performing persona. The real one. The one who never needed fixing. Just a little unlearning. Just a little space.

Let that be enough.

Living for Applause vs. Living With Peace

At some point, you start to feel the difference between the rush of being seen and the relief of being still. And that moment — that small, flickering shift — is where everything begins to change.

Living for applause is like being on a stage that never dims. Even when the show's over, you're backstage reapplying your makeup, wondering if you should've held that last note longer, analyzing why Row 3 didn't laugh. You start making choices not because they feel good, but because they'll land better. Because they photograph well. Because they'll get claps.

It's not always obvious. Sometimes applause-chasing looks like chronic overexplaining. Or posting something raw on social media and feeling mildly sick until it's met with sympathy. Or constantly second-guessing your tone in texts because what if they misunderstood and now they hate you forever?

You tell yourself it's just being conscientious. You call it thoughtfulness, responsibility, self-awareness. But really? It's a compulsion. It's the body trying to earn safety in a world where your worth always felt conditional.

Meanwhile, peace is over there in the corner — barefoot, kind of boring, very into herbal tea. Not chasing anything. Just existing. It doesn't get a standing ovation, but damn if it doesn't feel like oxygen after years of trying to prove your aliveness.

Peace is the moment you don't post. The reply you don't over-edit. The decision you make in your gut that doesn't come with a five-slide rationale. It's the walk you take without documenting it. It's choosing what makes you feel full, even if no one claps for it. Even if no one knows.

And here's the uncomfortable truth: If you've spent years living for applause, peace can feel like failure. Like you're not doing enough. Like you've disappeared. That's your nervous system detoxing from a lifetime of chasing visibility.

This isn't about going off-grid or becoming a monk (unless you want to, in which case — robe on). It's about making choices that are quieter, truer, less externally contorted. It's about asking, *"Would I still want this if no one ever knew?"

That question alone can break a thousand invisible chains.

Peace doesn't perform. It doesn't audition. It doesn't need the room to clap before it knows it belongs there.

And now you're left with this strange quiet. No claps. No gold stars. Just... you. You and your thoughts and your dinner in peace. You'll start noticing moments that used to fly past unnoticed — the kind of satisfaction that doesn't come with a dopamine spike or a social media hit. The kind that builds slowly, like moss. Subtle, grounded, ridiculously alive.

This is where you'll rediscover what peace actually feels like in your body. It's not passive. It's not boring. It's not some Zen monk hovering above the chaos. It's the steadiness you feel when you're no longer performing. The strength in not explaining and the badassery of keeping your joy to yourself without needing a single like for proof.

Living for applause trains you to seek adrenaline. Living with peace teaches you to seek alignment.

And it's not always obvious when the shift happens. You might still post the photo. Still write the caption. Still do the ambitious thing. But something inside is different. You're not doing it to be *seen*. You're doing it because it *feels right* — even if no one notices.

When you stop chasing validation, the volume of your own intuition goes up. And sometimes, that voice will say, "Rest." Or, "Don't post that." Or, "You don't need to go." And the old you might panic, thinking, *But they'll forget me. They'll think I'm lazy. They'll think I don't care.*

Let them.

Let them be wrong about you while you're right with yourself.

That's the real mic drop — not walking offstage, but ignoring the audience altogether and walking back *into your life*.

Quietly. Fully. Peacefully.

And not needing anyone to clap.

CHAPTER 11:

WHERE TO FROM HERE?

*Healing isn't a destination.
It's a relationship with yourself.*

So, Now What?

There's a strange sadness that creeps in after the breakthrough. Not the kind that knocks you flat, but the quiet, confusing kind — like walking into a house you once called home and realizing you no longer belong there.

You've let go of the perfectionist patterns. You've dropped the mask, peeled off the armor, stopped performing. You've rewritten your metrics for success, stopped chasing applause, stopped making your worth a group project. And now... what?

Now you grieve.

Grieve the version of you who tried so damn hard. Who spent years tap-dancing for approval, polishing every flaw, trying to earn safety in a world that kept moving the finish line. Grieve the identity that was built on striving, performing, and proving. The version of you who learned how to survive by overachieving. The version who believed that if they just did everything right, they'd finally get to exhale.

Grieve her. Grieve him. Grieve the hustle. Grieve the mask. Grieve the safety it gave you, even if it came at the cost of your joy.

Because even when the performance was exhausting, it was familiar. And there's a comfort in the known, even when it's a cage. When you begin to dismantle your perfectionist identity, you're not just changing habits — you're mourning a self you inhabited for years. A self who got you here.

You might feel unanchored. Like you don't know who you are without the constant measuring, comparing, fixing. That's not regression. That's rebirth. But before rebirth comes the grief — the letting go. And grief doesn't always look like sobbing into your pillow. Sometimes it looks like irritability. Like feeling lost. Like boredom. Like rage. Like watching Netflix for eight hours straight because you don't know what else to do with yourself.

This isn't a sign you're failing. It's a sign you're human.

We're not taught how to grieve the versions of ourselves we've outgrown. We're told to celebrate change — to sprint into the new with gratitude and excitement. But sometimes, healing feels like a funeral. And it should. That old version of you deserves to be honored. They worked hard. They tried. They kept you alive. And now... they're no longer needed.

The grief is proof that something real is happening.

So take your time. Light a candle if you want. Write a goodbye letter. Or don't. Just notice the ache. Let it speak. Let it pass. It's not asking you to go back. It's asking to be witnessed.

And once it softens — because it will — you'll begin to feel the space that grief leaves behind. A clearing. A possibility. A quiet sense of, *maybe I don't need to be anyone but me.*

And if you feel like you're about to swing too far, to blow it all up, to declare you're now a barefoot shaman who only eats mangoes on odd-numbered days — hold tight. That urge to rebel is just fear in a different outfit. We'll talk about that next.

Radical Self-Trust as the Final Goal

Letting go of perfectionism isn't the end. It's not the magical finish line where you wipe your forehead, post a carousel of your inner growth on Instagram, and start existing in some enlightened state of barefoot bliss and green smoothies. It's more like ripping the scaffolding off your house and realizing you don't know how to live in your own skin without it.

And the biggest mindfuck? That weird, disorienting space that opens up after you stop performing.

Because if I'm not performing anymore... who even am I?

Cue the identity panic. Cue the wildly swinging pendulum.

That's where many of us do one of two things:

We freeze or we flail.

Some freeze. We call it rest, but it's actually a collapse. An apathetic, soul-numbing inertia dressed up as "taking a break." And to be fair, a break *was* needed. But at some point, it stops being restorative and starts becoming a lifestyle. You go from burnout to blurry nothingness. You don't want to be seen, but you don't really want to disappear either. You just sort of... vanish in plain sight.

You stop reaching out. You stop showing up. You lie on the couch watching people live their lives through little squares while telling yourself you're above it all now. You've transcended the performance game. You're too evolved for goals or effort or caring. But if you're honest, you're also kind of miserable. You're drifting. And deep down, you know it.

Because rebelling against the system isn't the same thing as being free. Opting out of the rat race can still be a form of perfectionism—just reversed. Instead of striving to be everything, now you're striving to be nothing. And ironically, it's still not based on *choice*. It's a reaction. Not a rooted decision. You've gone from hyper-functioning to passive resistance, but you're still orbiting the same black hole: "Who am I if I'm not performing?"

Others flail. They don't collapse—they explode. Suddenly, every caption is chaotic. Every conversation is "real talk." Every outfit is a rebellion. They'll drop F-bombs in Zoom meetings and air their deepest traumas on social media. They're not just imperfect now—they're *loudly, radically, unapologetically* messy. And on the surface, it looks brave.

But underneath? It's sometimes panic in costume. A desperate grab at differentiation. If I can't win the game by being perfect, I'll burn the rulebook and dance on the ashes. I'll be so out there, so raw, so anti-perfect that nobody can accuse me of faking it ever again.

It's not coming from freedom. It's coming from fear.

And I get it. I did this in my early twenties—blurted out hot takes no one asked for, wore pain like an accessory, tried to be "deep" and "real" but mostly came across as rude, anxious, and vaguely exhausting. People didn't see me as liberated. They saw me as a walking red flag. Because I was performatively trying to prove I *wasn't* hiding anything.

Oh yeah? Well… I was hiding *everything*.

This isn't judgment. This is compassion for the messy middle. That weird, fumbling transition zone where you're trying not to go back to perfectionism but you haven't quite built trust in the alternative yet. So you pendulum swing. You overcorrect. And like any overcorrection, it's usually unstable. You are looking for yourself… and it's scary.

Radical self-trust, the kind you're really after, isn't found in apathy or performance. It's found in quiet consistency. In subtle knowing. It's the ability to hear your own voice and *believe* it, without asking five friends or posting a poll.

It's when you don't need to dramatically quit a job to know it's not for you. When you can take a break without turning it into an identity. When you can be messy without making it your brand.

And maybe most importantly? It's when you realize you don't have to be *seen* to be *valid*.

You're not here to prove anything anymore. Not that you're healed. Not that you're different. Not that you're edgy. Not that you're done.

You're just here. Breathing. Choosing. Returning.

Quietly doing what's right for you, because your gut says so.

And that's the beginning of true freedom.

The Quiet Miracle of Real Freedom

There will be a morning... maybe not the first one, but the first one you really *notice*... when you wake up and your chest isn't clenched. No cortisol jolt. No mental list stampeding through your brain like horses at the gate. Just... air. In. Out. Soft. Unremarkable. Holy.

You don't realize how much tension you were living with until it's gone. The hypervigilance. The teeth grinding. The stomach doing somersaults before emails even load. It's not that your life suddenly looks perfect. The dishes still need doing. Your skin's not airbrushed. Your to-do list didn't self-complete in the night like a loyal house elf. But your nervous system is no longer screaming that you're behind, that you're wrong, that you're failing some invisible test just by existing.

This is what freedom feels like... not a confetti moment, but a recalibrated *baseline*. Like slipping into water that's finally body temperature. Like realizing you no longer flinch when someone says "Can we talk?" Or walks past without smiling. Or critiques your work. You don't spiral, you don't shrink. You register it, and you keep breathing.

You laugh more. Not performative laughter, not the polite chuckle at something someone said in a meeting, but that wild, hiccupy kind that makes your shoulders shake. You cry easier, too. And the feel like releasing a pressure valve—honest, clean. They mean your body trusts you now.

You start reaching for clothes you *want* to wear, not ones that make you look more accomplished, thinner, trendier, less *you*. You don't rehearse conversations in your head before ordering coffee. You text back slower. You take longer to decide. You forget to apologize for taking up space.

Some days, it still sneaks back. The inner judge. The impulse to fix, perfect, improve. But it's quieter now. And you can meet it with a raised eyebrow and a soft internal whisper: "We don't do that anymore."

And people around you start to change too. Or maybe it's not them, maybe it's just your perception that shifts. You're no longer auditioning for their acceptance. So you see more clearly who loves you, not your performance. Who stays when you're soft. Who laughs when you're weird. Who sits with you, not out of obligation but comfort.

You forgive yourself faster. You spend less time post-morteming social interactions. You trust that silence isn't rejection, that disagreement isn't disaster, that being misunderstood doesn't mean you're unworthy. You rest without earning it. You succeed without needing to flaunt it. You fail without collapsing.

You look in the mirror and your first thought isn't "What needs fixing?" Sometimes, it's "God, I'm glad you're here."

This isn't some final state. It's not sainthood. It's not a badge you earn. It's a lived, breathing relationship with yourself. You'll mess it up. You'll forget. You'll regress. But you'll come back faster. And when you do, it's like finding your favorite song on the radio again. Familiar. Safe. Joyful.

Freedom is not loud or explosive. It won't post a transformation pic or make a viral TikTok. It's the slow, quiet rebuilding of trust with yourself. It's being able to hear your intuition without all the static. It's knowing that your value isn't in what you prove, but in what you *are*.

And what you are is finally, breathtakingly, enough.

So take the deeper breath. The one your body forgot it was allowed to take.

Exhale the old scripts.

Welcome the stillness.

This is what it feels like to be free.

CONCLUSION:

YOU WERE NEVER BROKEN

If you've made it here, to the very last page, take a breath. A real one. Let your shoulders drop. Let the noise fade for a second. You did something big. Not just because you read this whole book, but because you let it get in. You let yourself be seen—by you.

That's rare. And that's brave.

Perfectionism is sticky. It wraps itself around your worth, your identity, your story. It convinces you that your value is a moving target, that love must be earned, that safety is reserved for the flawless. But that was never true. You were never meant to be a goddamn performance.

Maybe you learned to hustle for love. Maybe you became hyper-capable so no one could criticize you. Maybe your armor is humor. Or silence. Or productivity. Or people-pleasing so expertly done it almost looks like kindness.

And maybe you're just tired.

That's the word I hear the most when people describe their perfectionism: exhausted. Tired of proving. Tired of shrinking. Tired of spinning in circles chasing gold stars that melt the second you touch them.

So if you're here hoping for one final life-changing insight, I won't give you that. Not because there isn't one—but because you don't need one. You don't need to chase another "aha." You don't need to fix yourself. The truth is quieter, and harder to market:

You are not a self-improvement project.

You are a person. Glorious. Complicated. In progress. And so, so worthy.

Maybe you'll re-read this book someday. Maybe you'll dog-ear a chapter, or screenshot a line, or shove it into a friend's hands and say "This. Read this." But I hope, more than anything, that when you put it down, you walk away a little lighter. A little less afraid. A little more you.

And on the days you slip? Because you will. We all do. Come back. Not to the rules. Not to the hustle. Not to the pressure. Come back to you.

You are allowed to rest.

You are allowed to show up undone.

You are allowed to be human here.

This is your life. Not a performance. Not a dress rehearsal. Not a test.

And my god, it's beautiful when it's messy.

You were never broken. Just buried under layers of "should."

You get to come home now.

Author's Note

I didn't write this book from a mountaintop.

There's no halo above my head, no perfect morning routine, no "fully healed" badge on my jacket. I still catch myself spiraling when I feel unseen. I still overcompensate. I still sometimes open social media and compare myself to people I don't even *like*.

But I wrote this book anyway.

Because I needed to say what I wish someone had told *me* earlier. I needed to put words to the aching pressure that so many of us carry quietly—people who look "together" on the outside but feel like they're quietly crumbling inside from all the proving, all the pleasing, all the pretending.

If that's you? You're not alone.

You're not dramatic, or lazy, or weak. You're not "too sensitive." You're just someone who's been running on empty for too long, trying to earn something that should have been yours from the beginning: safety, rest, joy, acceptance.

This book is my offering. Not as a blueprint, but as a reminder: it's okay to be undone, and it's okay to slack off once in a while. You don't have to become a different person to be loved. You don't have to fix everything before you're allowed to exhale.

Your softness is not a flaw. Your mess is not a disqualification. Your humanity is not a liability.

That's the whole point.

If something in these pages cracked you open, even a little… I'm grateful. If it pissed you off, even better. Growth has a way of being annoying before it feels beautiful. But if nothing else, I hope this book gave you permission to stop trying so hard to be perfect, and start being *real*.

You deserve a life that fits *you*, not just the version of you that other people applaud.

Thank you for being here.

Keep going. Grant the world with the real you.

Fiercely yours,
Tali

YOU MADE IT HERE. AND THAT MAKES YOU PART OF THE SOLUTION.

If you've reached this page, you've already done something most people never attempt: you looked perfectionism in the eye and refused to be ruled by it.

Now you get to do something even more powerful.

You can help someone else escape it.

Books like this travel from hand to hand because a reader steps up and says, *"This helped me. It might help you too."*

That simple act changes the landscape far beyond algorithms and rankings.

It tells people who are drowning in pressure, self-criticism, and impossible standards that relief exists, and that someone out there cared enough to show them the way.

If you're willing to be that person, the quiet hero in someone else's turning point, tap the QR code and leave a short review. It doesn't need to be poetic. It just needs to be yours.

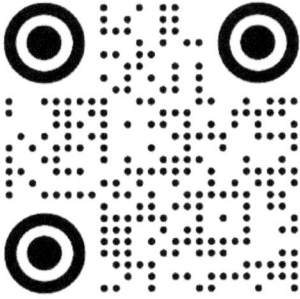

And if you want to stay connected, get early releases, vote on future book topics, or read new pages before anyone else, join the mailing list below.

You didn't just finish a book.

You contributed to a movement where imperfect humans finally get to breathe, create, love, and live without fear.

Thanks for leading the way.

References

Brené Brown. (2012). *Daring greatly: How the courage to be vulnerable transforms the way we live, love, parent, and lead.* Avery.

Brown, B. (2015). *Rising strong: How the ability to reset transforms the way we live, love, parent, and lead.* Spiegel & Grau.

Fosha, D. (2000). *The transforming power of affect: A model for accelerated change.* Basic Books.

Gilbert, P. (2010). *Compassion focused therapy: Distinctive features.* Routledge.

Gottman, J., & Silver, N. (2015). *The seven principles for making marriage work: A practical guide from the country's foremost relationship expert.* Harmony Books.

Horney, K. (1950). *Neurosis and human growth: The struggle toward self-realization.* W. W. Norton.

Maté, G. (2003). *When the body says no: Exploring the stress-disease connection.* Wiley.

Neff, K. D. (2011). *Self-compassion: The proven power of being kind to yourself.* William Morrow.

Porges, S. W. (2011). *The polyvagal theory: Neurophysiological foundations of emotions, attachment, communication, and self-regulation.* W. W. Norton.

Rogers, C. R. (1961). *On becoming a person: A therapist's view of psychotherapy.* Houghton Mifflin.

Schwartz, R. C. (2021). *No bad parts: Healing trauma and restoring wholeness with the Internal Family Systems model.* Sounds True.

Siegel, D. J. (2010). *The mindful therapist: A clinician's guide to mindsight and neural integration.* W. W. Norton.

Stutz, P., & Michels, J. (2022). *The tools: Transform your problems into courage, confidence, and creativity.* Spiegel & Grau.

Tolle, E. (1997). *The power of now: A guide to spiritual enlightenment.* New World Library.

Van der Kolk, B. (2014). *The body keeps the score: Brain, mind, and body in the healing of trauma.* Viking.

Young, J. E., Klosko, J. S., & Weishaar, M. E. (2003). *Schema therapy: A practitioner's guide.* Guilford Press.